Pavilion

by Emily White

The world premiere of *Pavilion* took place at Theatr Clwyd
on 26 September 2019.

Cast   In alphabetical order

Ifan Huw Dafydd	Dewi
Carly-Sophia Davies	Jess
Caitlin Drake	Myfanwy
Elis Duffy	Gary
Michael Geary	Evan
Lowri Hamer	Bethan
Victoria John	Big Nell
Kristian Phillips	Lloyd
Adam Redmore	Mark/Will
Rebecca Smith-Williams	Mary/Catrin
Tim Treloar	Dylan

Community Cast

Vanessa Owen | Emily Roberts | Joshua Roberts | Hannah Swain
Ben Wheelhouse | Sadie Shantelle Williams

Creative Team

Writer	Emily White
Director	Tamara Harvey
Designer	Jacob Hughes
Lighting Designer	Tim Mascall
Sound Designer	Dan Balfour
Choreographer	Annie-Lunnette Deakin Foster
Fight Director	Owain Gwynn
Assistant Director	Francesca Goodridge
Theatr Clwyd Carne Traineeship	
Movement (support)	Angharad Jones
Music (support)	Aled Marshman
Company Stage Manager	Harriet Stewart
Deputy Stage Manager	Amber Chapell
Assistant Stage Manager	Sarah Barnes
Casting Director	Annelie Powell
Casting Assistant	Lilly Mackie
Writers in Residence	Ming Ho	Hefin Robinson
Supported by Gladstone's Library	
Producer	William James
Production Manager	Jim Davies
Costume Supervisor	Debbie Knight

Ifan Huw Dafydd

Ifan Huw Dafydd plays Dewi. His previous theatre credits for Theatr Clwyd include *Under Milk Wood*, *As You Like It*, *Blackthorn*, *Festen*, *History of Falling Things*, *The Drawer Boy*, *Memory*, *King Lear*. Other theatre credits include *The Wood* (Torch Theatre), *Raving* (Hampstead Theatre), *Desire Line* (Sherman Theatre), and *An Enemy For The People* (Chapter Arts Centre), *The Dark Earth and the Light Sky* (Almeida). For television, his credits include *The Light*, *4 Stories: On The Edge*, *Pitching In*, *15 Days*, *The Crown*, awarded BAFTA for Jac in *Martha, Jac a Sianco*.

Carly-Sophia Davies

Carly-Sophia Davies plays Jess. She graduated from LAMDA in 2018. Her credits include *A Midsummer Night's Dream* and *I Love You, You're Perfect, Now Change* (Taliesin Theatre).

Caitlin Drake

Caitlin Drake plays Myfanwy. She graduated from Italia Conti in 2019. This marks her professional debut.

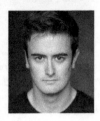

Ellis Duffy

Ellis Duffy plays Gary. He trained at Bristol Old Vic Theatre School. His previous theatre credits include *Scrapper* (Theatre West), *13* (Tobacco Factory) and *Dead Born Grow* (Frantic Assembly at Aberystwyth Arts Centre).

Lowri Hamer

Lowri Hamer plays Bethan. She trained in Musical Theatre at GSA. Her previous theatre credits include *Salad Days* (New Union Theatre and Theatre Royal, Bath) and *Lord of the Flies* (Theatr Clwyd and Sherman Theatre).

Michael Geary

Michael Geary plays Evan. His previous credits for Theatr Clwyd include *Orpheus Descending*, *My People*, *The Light of Heart*, *Rape of the Fair Country*, *As You Like It*, *Humbug*, *Taking Steps*, *The Taming of the Shrew*, *A Child's Christmas in Wales*, *Tall Tales*, *Thinking Out Loud*, *Festen*, *A Midsummer Night's Dream*, *Tales from Small Nations* and *The Suicide*. Other theatre credits include *The Boy Who Fell into a Book* (Soho Theatre), *The Merry Wives of Windsor* (Guildford Shakespeare Company) and *Fantastic Mr Fox* (Regent's Park Open Air Theatre). For film, his credits include *Viking Siege*, *Tulip Fever* and *The Baker*.

Victoria John

Victoria John plays Big Nell. Her previous credits for Theatr Clwyd include *Wave Me Goodbye*, *The Rise and Fall of Little Voice*, *Cyrano de Bergerac*, *All My Sons*, *The Light of Heart*, *Aristocrats*, *The Winslow Boy*, *Rape of the Fair Country* and *Boeing Boeing*. Other theatre credits include *Hir* (Bush Theatre), *Play* (The Other Room) and *The Frozen Scream* (Wales Millennium Centre, Birmingham Hippodrome). For television, her credits include *Gwaith/Cartref*, *Miranda*, *Cast Offs* and *Little Britain*.

Kristian Phillips

Kristian Phillips plays Lloyd. His previous work for the company includes *Season's Greetings* and *Bruised*. His other theatre credits include *As You Like It* (Regent's Park Open Air Theatre), *Richard III* (Almeida Theatre), *Of Mice and Men* (Birmingham Rep, UK tour), *The Alchemist* (Liverpool Playhouse), *The Sea Plays* (Old Vic Tunnels), *Crazy Gary's Mobile Disco* (Tron and Traverse Theatre) and *The Passion* (National Theatre of Wales). For television, his credits include *Shakespeare & Hathaway: Private Investigators*, *Press*, *Nightmares* and *Wizards vs Aliens*.

Adam Redmore

Adam Redmore plays Mark/Will. His previous theatre credits include *Sugar Baby* (Edinburgh Festival Fringe), *Wonderman* (National Theatre Wales), *Milked* (UK tour), *Roberto Zucco* (Chapter Arts), *Maudie's Rooms, Clytemnestra* (Sherman Theatre), *Tonypandemonium* (National Theatre Wales) and *Caligula* (Chapter Arts).

Rebecca Smith-Williams

Rebecca Smith-Williams plays Mary. Her previous work for the company includes *Humbug.* Her previous theatre credits include *Y Brain/Kargalar* (Be Aware productions), *The Eyes Have It* (Watford Palace Theatre), *Darkness Spoken* (Southbank Centre), *Othello* (Chester Grosvenor Park *Black Battles with Dogs* (Southwark Playhouse), *After Troy* (Oxford Playhouse), *The Fool* (Cock Tavern) and *Mary Mother of Frankenstein* (The National Theatre of Belgium) and with her own company Triangl; *Margaret and the Tapeworm* (Chapter Arts Centre, UK tour), *Miramar* (UK tour).

Tim Treloar

Tim Treloar plays Dylan. His previous theatre credits include *Birdsong, Wait Until Dark* (UK tours), *House/ Garden* (The Watermill Theatre), *The Heart of Robin Hood, Thomas More, Sejanus, Believe What you Will, Richard 3rd, Romeo & Juliet, Back to Methuselah* (Royal Shakespeare Company), *Three Sisters* (Lyric Belfast), *King Charles 3rd* (Sydney Theatre Company), *A Midsummer Night's Dream* (Squerryes Court), *I Kiss your Heart, Realism* (Soho Theatre), *Macbeth* (West End and Broadway), *King Lear* (Chichester and New York), *Twelfth Night* (Chichester), *Mountain Language* (Royal Court), *Rose Rage* (West End), *Henry V* (National Theatre), *The Duchess of Malfi, Volpone, Dr Fautus, School for Scandal* (Greenwich Theatre), *Beggars Opera* (Orange Tree). Television includes; *The Tuckers, Call the Midwife, Dark Heart, Cross Liner, Father Brown, Holby City, Mammon, The Bill, Mayday, Liquid Bomb Plot, Doctors, Framed, Silent Witness, A Touch of Frost, Casualty, Bombshell, The Brief, Foyler War, Bomber, Single, The Bench, Midsomer Murders.* Film includes; *The Voyage of Dr Dolittle, A Hundred Streets, Maleficent, The Crown and The Dragon, Macbeth, Wondrous, Oblivion.* Tim is the winner of the BBL Carleton Hobbs Award and is The Third Doctor Who for Big Finish.

Emily White | Writer

Emily originally trained as an actress at RADA many moons ago before obtaining an MA in Theatre Writing at York University. She left with a hangover and a distinction and hasn't stopped writing since.

In 2018 she was selected to be one of 12 writers to take part in the Channel 4's 4Screenwriting Course and this year she was selected to be part of the BBC Wales Writersroom group. She is currently developing projects for TV, theatre and film and is writing a digital theatre piece for Wrapt Films/Open Sky Theatre. *Pavilion* is her debut production as a writer.

Tamara Harvey | Director

Tamara Harvey has been Artistic Director of Theatr Clwyd since August 2015. Most recently she directed *Orpheus Descending* in co-production with the Menier Chocolate Factory and the première of *Home, I'm Darling* by Laura Wade, nominated for UK Theatre and Evening Standard Awards, as well as five Olivier Awards, winning the Olivier for Best New Comedy, and transferring to the West End before returning to Clwyd. Also for the company she has directed *Much Ado About Nothing*, the première of Elinor Cook's award-winning play, *Pilgrims, Skylight* by David Hare and the première of Peter Gill's version of *Uncle Vanya* (Best Production, Best Supporting Actress and Best Director in the English Language at the Wales Theatre Awards). She was previously a freelance director, working in the West End, throughout the UK and abroad, on classic plays, new writing, musical theatre and in film.

Her previous credits include the world premières of *From Here to Eternity* (Shaftesbury Theatre), *Breeders* (St James Theatre), *The Kitchen Sink, The Contingency Plan, Sixty-Six Books* and *tHe dYsFUnCKshOnalZ!* (Bush Theatre), *In the Vale of Health* (a cycle of four plays by Simon Gray), *Elephants* and *Hello/Goodbye* (Hampstead Theatre), *Plague Over England* (Finborough Theatre & West End). Other theatre includes *Kreutzer vs Kreutzer* (Sam Wanamaker Playhouse/Royal Festival Hall), *Bash* (Trafalgar Studios), *Whipping It Up* (New Ambassadors), *One Flew Over the Cuckoo's Nest* (Gielgud & Garrick Theatres), *Educating Rita* (Menier Chocolate Factory & Theatre Royal Bath), the UK première of *Something Cloudy, Something Clear* (Finborough Theatre) and *Pride and Prejudice* (Sheffield Theatres).

Jacob Hughes | Designer

Jacob graduated from the Royal Welsh College of Music and Drama in 2011 and was a finalist in the Linbury Prize for Stage Design that same year. He has since been nominated for Best Set Designer in the Off West End Awards, Wales Theatre Awards and has exhibited his work in the Society of British Theatre Designers exhibition *Make:Believe*. In 2016 Jacob became the National Theatre's first recipient of the Max Rayne Design Bursary Award.

Design credits include: *Tales Of The Turntable* (ZooNation), *Poet In Da Corner* (Royal Court), *The Rise And Fall Of Little Voice* (Park Theatre), *Dusty The Musical* (associate, West End & UK Tour), *Twilight: Los Angeles 1992* (Gate Theatre), *Broad Shadow* (associate, National Theatre), *Start Swimming* (Young Vic), *War Whores* (Courtyard Theatre), *Un Ballo In Maschera, Il Trovatore* (Winslow Hall Opera), *Manon Lescaut* (Royal Opera House), *Mr Swallow: Houdini* (Soho Theatre), *The Island, Mojo* (LAMDA), *Mydidae, The Prince of Homburg, Copenhagen, Lift Off* (Linbury Studio, LAMDA), *Napoleon Blown Apart* (Arcola Theatre), *Sexual Perversity In Chicago* (Sherman Cymru & national tour), *Not The Messiah* (Leicester Square Theatre, Theatre503), *The Aeniad* (Oxford Playhouse), *King Lear* (Royal Welsh College of Music and Drama).

Tim Mascall | Lighting Designer

Tim is a Lighting Designer for Theatre, Opera and Dance and has designed extensively in the West End, across the UK and internationally. Previously for Theatr Clwyd he designed for *Orpheus Descending* and *Lord Of The Flies* in 2018.

Other companies he has designed for include: National Theatre of Scotland, Royal Lyceum, Edinburgh, Dundee Rep, Complicité, Theatre Royal Bath, Menier Chocolate Factory, Rose Theatre, Kingston and many others.

Opera credits include: *The Cunning Little Vixen* (Garsington), *Aida* (Opera Holland Park) and *Peter Grimes and The Gamblers* (Royal Festival Hall).

Annie-Lunnette Deakin Foster | Choreographer

Annie-Lunnette Deakin-Foster is a passionate contemporary dance theatre choreographer, maker and movement director, and was a co-founding member of award winning company, C-12 Dance Theatre.

She previously worked for Theatr Clwyd and Paines Plough in the ROUNDABOUT season on *Daughterhood* by Charley Miles, *On The Other Hand We're Happy* by Daf James, and *Dexter & Winter's Detective Agency* by Nathan Byron dir. by Stef Driscoll. Recent theatre credits include: *Chiaroscuro* by Jackie Kay dir. by Lynette Linton at The Bush; *Aesop's Fables* by Justin Audibert and Rachel Bagshaw at the Unicorn Theatre; *You Stupid Darkness* by Sam Steiner directed by James Grieve at The Theatre Royal Plymouth; *Grimm Tales* Phillip Pullman's collection adapted by Philip Wilson directed by Kirsty Housley at the Unicorn Theatre; *Jericho's Rose* by Althea Theatre at The Hope & Anchor; *POP MUSIC* by Anna Jordan and directed by James Grieve, Barry Jackson and national tour; *The Court Must Have a Queen* by Ade Solanke directed by Sam Curtis Lindsay at Hampton Court Palace; *These Bridges* by Phoebe Éclair-Powell (WCYT as part of National Theatre Connections at The Bush); *The Little Match Girl and Other Happier Tales* by Joel Horwood and Emma Rice (2016-2017 Shakespeare's Globe and presented by Bristol Old Vic 2017-2018 then toured nationally). *The Dark Room* by Angela Betzien (Theatre 503).

Recent dance credits include: *Force* (Abbey Road Studios, Imagine Festival Watford, Greenwich & Docklands International Festival, & Netherlands), *Shhh!* (Dance City, MAC Birmingham, Norwich Playhouse, The Woodville Gravesend, CircoMedia Bristol, Winchester Theatre Royal)

Owain Gwynn | Fight Director

Owain trained on the Acting and Stage Combat degree at East15. He has since gained numerous credits as an actor both on stage and screen, alongside which he has worked consistently as a fight director and consultant on a variety of productions. His work includes:

As fight director: *Life Of Pi* (Sheffield Theatres); *Cymbeline* (Sam Wanamaker Theatre / Shakespeare's Globe); *The Homecoming* (Trafalgar Studios / Jamie Lloyd Productions); *Macbeth* (Young Vic Theatre); *Medea* (National Theatre); *Billy Liar* (Manchester Royal Exchange); *Jekyll And Hyde, Superior Donuts* (Southwark Playhouse); *Pigeons* (The Royal Court); *Wozzeck* (English National Opera); *Y Tad* (Theatr Genedlaethol Cymru - Welsh National Theatre)

As Assistant Fight Director: *Macbeth* (Trafalgar Studios / Jamie Lloyd Productions); *Warhorse* (West End / National Theatre)

As Fight Consultant/Captain: *Peter Pan, Porgy and Bess* (Regent's Park Open Air Theatre); *Hamlet* (Theatr Clwyd); *The Light Princess* (National Theatre); *Macbeth, Deffro'r Gwanwyn* (Theatr Genedlaethol Cymru - Welsh National Theatre)

Dan Balfour | Sound Designer

Dan is a London based Sound Designer and Dramaturg. His recent work includes: *HOME* (Young Vic), *Counting Sheep* (Belarus Free Theatre), *hang* (Sheffield Crucible), *Wilderness* (Hampstead Theatre), *Operation Mincemeat* (New Diorama Theatre), *ILLEGALISED, VINOVAT, -Ä* (Bezna Theatre), *LAVA* (Nottingham Playhouse); *Effigies Of Wickedness* (Gate Theatre); *Great Apes* (Arcola Theatre), *Spindrift* (Curious Directive), *Cymbeline, The Devils, The Rover* (RCSSD).

Associate Sound Design includes: *Fanny & Alexander* (Old Vic), *The Lorax* (Old Vic Toronto Tour), *People Places & Things* (Headlong), *There Is A Light That Never Goes Out* (Manchester Royal Exchange), *Oresteia* (Almeida Theatre), *Life Of Galileo* (Young Vic),

Dan is a current Off Westend Award, Best Sound Design nominee for his work on *Operation Mincemeat* (New Diorama) and was nominated twice in 2018 for his work on *Great Apes* (Arcola) and *Blood Wedding* (Omnibus). Dan is the Company Sound Designer for the British-Romanian theatre company, Bezna Theatre

Franscesca Goodridge | Assistant Director
(Theatr Clwyd Carne Traineeship)

Francesca Goodridge trained at Liverpool Institute for Performing Arts (LIPA) achieving a BA Hons in Acting. She is now one of the two directors of Theatr Clwyd's Carne Traineeship for Directors in Wales. Francesca has experience as an actor, vocalist, choreographer and director, she is the former Trainee Director of The Other Room Theatre in Cardiff.

Thanks

Lynda at We Three Loggerheads | Kim at the Royal Exchange Theatre Glasfryn | Tom at Lime Pictures | Paul at Captain Haddock Fish & Chips

The award-winning Theatr Clwyd is Wales' biggest producing theatre.

Based in Flintshire, the gateway to North Wales, since 1976 Theatr Clwyd has been a cultural powerhouse producing world-class theatre, from the UK Theatre Award-winning musical *The Assassination Of Katie Hopkins* and National Theatre and West End Olivier award-winning comedy *Home, I'm Darling*, to the site specific, immersive *The* Great Gatsby and its sell-out rock 'n' roll pantomimes.

Led by Artistic Director Tamara Harvey and Executive Director Liam Evans-Ford, Theatr Clwyd's world-class team of workshop, wardrobe and scenic artists, props makers and technicians ensure the skills vital to a vibrant theatre industry are nurtured right in the heart of Wales.

Alongside the three theatre spaces, cinema, café, bar and art galleries, Theatr Clwyd works with the community in many different guises across all art forms and is recognised as a cultural leader for its cross-generational theatre groups, work in youth justice and diverse programme of arts, health and wellbeing.

Find out more: www.theatrclwyd.com
Twitter: @ClwydTweets
Follow Us: Facebook.com/TheatrClwyd

Pavilion

Emily White is an emerging screenwriter and playwright. She trained as an actress at RADA before taking an MA in Theatre Writing at the University of York, for which she received a distinction. In 2018 she won a place on Channel 4's 4Screenwriting Course where she developed her pilot *Land of My Fathers* about a Syrian refugee coming to live in a small Welsh town. She was then selected to be part of the BBC Wales Writersroom group in 2019. She is also writing a digital theatre piece for Wrapt Films/Open Sky Theatre and is part of a developmental writers room for a Bad Wolf television production in Cardiff. *Pavilion* received its world premiere at Theatr Clwyd in September 2019.

Myfanwy Alright I'll open up. Okay? Chips, burgers whatever you want, you won't even have to pay . . . alright?

Lloyd I'm not hungry for chips no more.

Lloyd punches Gary in the stomach and he crumples to the ground. Myfanwy runs to him and tries to shield him.

Myfanwy No! Leave him be!

Will pulls her away and holds her back. Lloyd kicks Gary in the face.

Help! Someone! Evan?! Nelly?!

Will covers Myfanwy's mouth and Lloyd continues to beat Gary who lies curled up on the ground, whimpering.

Will Enough, Lloyd. He's had enough.

Will tries to stop Lloyd. Lloyd punches Will, who reels backwards and falls to the ground stunned.

Stop, man! You'll kill him!

Lloyd What fuckin' difference does it make?!

Will You'll go to prison!

Lloyd What if I do?! Eh?! Eh?! Life in there will be better than it is out here! We're all fucked, mun! No matter what we do, we're all fucked!

Lloyd gets ready to close in on Gary again, but Will grabs a wooden post that's lying on the ground and hits him over the head with it. Lloyd collapses; his head bleeding. He hits him again; hard.
Silence. Gary does not move.

Myfanwy Gary!

She runs to him.

Gary? Wake up, love. Gary? Oh no. No.

She cradles Gary in her arms. Will just stands there, unsure what to do.

Dewi
And honoured among foxes and pheasants by the gay
house
Under the new made clouds and happy as the heart
was long,
In the sun born over and over,
I ran my heedless ways –

Music: 'Ghosts I' by Nine Inch Nails. The lights change and as Gary speaks the cast lift him up, carry him and place him on top of the bar, to look down at himself. As his speech continues the cast surround him and recite the poem from their places within the bar.

Gary The countdown has begun. Ten, nine, eight, seven . . . fear in my belly . . . six, five, four . . . knotted intestines hardening against each blow. I look up. I look up and I will myself to fly.

Dewi
My wishes raced through the house-high hay –

Gary Fly out of here just like in dreams. Three, two, one.

Dewi
And nothing I cared, at my sky blue trades, that time
allows
In all his tuneful turning so few and such morning
songs.

Big Nell
Before the children green and golden
Follow him out of grace.

EMILY WHITE

Pavilion

FABER & FABER

First published in 2019
by Faber and Faber Limited
74–77 Great Russell Street, London WC1B 3DA

First published 2019

Typeset by Country Setting, Kingsdown, Kent CT14 8ES
Printed in England by CPI Group (UK) Ltd, Croydon CR0 4YY

A CIP record for this book is available from the British Library

ISBN 978-0-571-35934-9

FSC
www.fsc.org
MIX
Paper from
responsible sources
FSC® C013604

2 4 6 8 10 9 7 5 3 1

For Dad

theatre was my first love,
thank you for introducing us

ACKNOWLEDGEMENTS

Special thanks should go to: Lloyd Trott and Stephen Darcy for their help with the development of the play, along with all the actors that were involved at various stages of its development at RADA. Raphael Martin for his literary advice and encouragement. The late, great Stephen Jeffreys for listening to my original pitch and saying: 'Hmm, this sounds like a play that needs to take place over the space of one evening.' The Dylan Thomas Trust for granting me the permission to use 'Fern Hill'. And of course, Tamara Harvey, everyone at Theatr Clwyd and all the actors in the cast for helping me realise my wildest dreams.

Author's Notes

With the exception of the Welsh songs, all songs included in the stage directions are suggestions only. Please feel free to choose different ones.

The company can double up roles as creatively as the director sees fit. For example the actor that plays Mark can also play Will, the actor playing Gary can also play the DJ, the actress playing Mary can also play Catrin, etc. Equally all actors can be on stage throughout and dip in and out of scenes as different characters.

All the characters have thick Welsh accents except for Catrin who has a softer Welsh accent.

A dash (–) at the end of a sentence denotes an interruption by another character.

An ellipsis (. . .) at the end of a sentence denotes a trailing off.

An elipsis (. . .) instead of a sentence denotes that the character is speechless for some reason.

A forward slash (/) denotes the overlapping of dialogue.

Pavilion was first performed at Theatr Clwyd, Mold, on 26 September 2019. The cast was as follows:

Jess Carly-Sophia Davies
Dewi Ifan Huw Dafydd
Myfanwy Caitlin Drake
Gary Ellis Duffy
Evan Michael Geary
Bethan Lowri Hamer
Big Nell Victoria John
Lloyd Kristian Phillips
Mark / Will Adam Redmore
Mary / Catrin Rebecca Smith-Williams
Dylan Tim Treloar

Director Tamara Harvey
Designer Jacob Hughes
Choreographer/Movement Annie-Lunnette Deakin-Foster
Lighting Designer Tim Mascall
Sound Designer Dan Balfour
Fight Director Owain Gwynne

Characters

Mark,
twenty-six, unemployed

Myfanwy
nineteen, chip van employee

Gary
sixteen, Jess's brother, cousin to Mary and Bethan,
secondary school student

Jess
eighteen, Gary's sister, cousin to Mary and Bethan,
secondary school student

Mary
twenty-six, Bethan's sister, a temp in London

Bethan
sixteen, Mary's sister, secondary school student, pregnant

Evan
fifties, barman

Dewi
sixty-one, from Merthyr Tydfil, ex-miner,
unemployed drunk

Big Nell
forties, barmaid

Dylan
forties, a history teacher and social activist

Lloyd
twenty-six, unemployed

Will
twenty-six, unemployed

Catrin
thirties, head teacher at the secondary school

DJ Smudge
and other small characters

Time

February 2016.

Place

A small town in Wales.

Design

If the space permits the play would work well
as a promenade performance involving the audience
as much as possible. Otherwise I would suggest
the bar could be at the back of the space facing the
audience. The space in front of the bar becomes the
dance floor, the toilets and the outdoor space in which
the moveable framework of a chip van is wheeled.

Act One

SCENE ONE

Winter. An old Victorian spa town in Wales. A grotty chip van stands outside of the local Friday-night disco, which is held in an old Pavilion; once a grand theatre, now a crumbling old hall with the seats pulled out to make way for a dance floor. There are posters pasted all over the front of the Pavilion that read PAVILION CLOSING. JOIN US FOR THE FINAL FRIDAY NIGHT DISCO WITH DJ SMUDGE.

Lights and music: 'Omen' by The Prodigy at full blast; the stage fills with people dancing like maniacs. The song tempo shifts, and out of the chaos steps Big Nell into a pool of light; the music shifts down a notch and she belts out her speech directly to the audience.

Big Nell Another Friday night in our dreary little hillside town. A Friday like every other spanning over the last thirty years. Not much changes round here. A quaint Victorian spa town on the face of it but there is something rancid and festering at its heart that cannot be denied. The beauty of this place is fading, replaced by rot and stink; derelict mansion flats crumble into the darkness and the surrounding housing estates are closing in.

It is a dark, damp, moonless night, harsh winds and a cold that cuts right through to your bones so that your hands and feet go blue with it.

A bunch of drunk girls stumble past. Nell introduces them.

The girls are out: no coat, no tights and not much of anything else either. Fake-tanned up to the nines; faces plastered in make-up, tottering down the icy streets in

11

their sky-high heels, pissed out of their fucking minds and looking for love in all the wrong places.

A bunch of drunk lads approach the girls. They interact and get turned away.

And here come the lads all beery and leery to meet them: frustrated big bundles of impotent rage determined to fight or fuck all that jobless anger out of themselves before the night is through.

Dewi crosses the dance floor, unsteady on his feet and trying not to spill a pint of beer.

And there are the old-timers, the pisshead regulars, the under-age teens jostling for an illegal tipple; egged on by their friends. And uh-oh, there may be trouble ahead: here come two Bristol boys like a couple of sore thumbs just waiting to be broken.

The Bristol boys cross the dance floor, watched closely by the rest of the cast.

They all convene at this place, the local Friday-night disco, the Pavilion or 'Pivvy': once a grand theatre for the upper echelons, now a draughty old cavernous wasteland for the hoi polloi. I've seen more blood, puke and tears than anyone should ever have to and I'm back every Friday night to witness more.

But this is it! Our last night open and lucky you, you're here to observe the proceedings for posterity. If you need some proof that human beings are no better than wild animals, then stick around. The night is young: let the mating rituals begin!

The music comes back full blast, everyone rocks out and then the music and lights are cut dead.

Blackout.

SCENE TWO

7.00 p.m. Myfanwy is setting up the chip van for business. As she works she sings the famous Welsh hymn, 'Calon Lân'. Gary enters and sits down to watch her.

Myfanwy
Nid wy'n gofyn bywyd moethus,
Aur y byd na'i berlau mân:
Gofyn wyf am galon hapus,
Calon onest, calon lân.

Mark enters and watches her.

Calon lân yn llawn daioni,
Tecach yw na'r lili dlos:
Dim ond calon lân all ganu –
Canu'r dydd a chanu'r nos.

Mark Gorgeous!

Myfanwy Christ! You scared me!

Mark Sorry, love. Serious though, you've the voice of an angel.

Myfanwy Sneaky bugger.

Mark You were like a siren calling my name.

Myfanwy Oh get to fuck.

Mark So . . . uh . . . what you doin' after?

Myfanwy Huh?

Mark Do you uh . . . fancy . . .?

Myfanwy What?

Mark You know . . . uh . . .

He wiggles his eyebrows, whistles and gyrates his hips.

Myfanwy Are you jokin' me or what? Look, um . . . Mark, that was strictly a one-time thing. Okay?

Mark Windy.

Myfanwy Sorry?

Mark My name. It's Windy.

Myfanwy What?! No it's not.

Mark Alright, nickname.

Myfanwy Serious? Why? No actually I don't wanna know.

Mark It's not so bad a nickname. One of my best mates is called Scrotum.

   Myfanwy laughs.

You've got a filthy laugh, Myfanwy.

Myfanwy Call me Miv. I hate Myfanwy.

Mark Well, Miv, I must say you look a vision this evening.

Myfanwy Oh get to fuck, you!

Mark No, truly. You really know how to rock a hairnet and that apron is accentuating your assets like you wouldn't believe. Only a true beauty could pull it off and you my lovely, look fuckin' *lush*!

Myfanwy Lush? Whatever. With my greasy chip-fat face.

Mark It makes your skin glow. Radiant like the moon.

Myfanwy You're a fuckin' nutter you are.

Mark So level with me, Miv my love, did we not have a fantastic night together?

Myfanwy It was okay.

Mark No, no, Miv, don't toy with my emotions, the truth now.

Myfanwy It was okay.

Mark Well I don't know what to say, Miv, but I'm gutted. I open myself up to you, vulnerable as a new-born lamb separated from its mother; I bare my soul to you and all I get back is 'okay'.

Myfanwy Oh Jesus Christ, alright! It was . . . quite good.

Mark Good?! It was *magnificent*!

Myfanwy Look I'm supposed to be working so –

Mark I'll help you!

He runs around the back of the van and gets in.

Myfanwy What? No!

Mark Oh come on, you'll need the help when the Pivvy empties out.

Myfanwy No. No.

Mark Miv, Miv, Mivvy, we don't know each other that well yet, but you'll soon learn that I am not a man that takes no for an answer.

Myfanwy You'll get me in trouble.

Mark You must learn to live life on the edge, Miv. Seize the day! Forever is composed of nows.

Myfanwy What does that mean?

Mark It means for one glorious night, throw caution to the wind! God, that hairnet makes me wanna give you one!

He grabs her and pulls her to him.

Myfanwy (*laughing*) Get off me! Someone might see!

Mark Let them! I must have you and I must have you now!

He nibbles at her neck and ears. She likes this.

Myfanwy Oh . . . mm . . . mmm . . . Oh fuck it.

Myfanwy grabs him and they disappear behind the counter. Laughter.
Gary wanders up to the van. He is dressed scruffily, nothing quite fits him properly and there are holes in his shoes.

Gary Miv? You there? Chips please . . .

Miv pops up looking slightly dishevelled.

Myfanwy Gary! What can I do you for?

Gary Er . . . chips?

Myfanwy Oh terribly sorry, Gary love, they're not in the fryer yet. Come back in ten.

She flips the catch and the hatch closes. Laughter and a 'Phwoar' from Mark are heard. The van begins to rock.

SCENE THREE

7.00 p.m. Inside the Pavilion bar, which is through a door to the side of the dance hall. Evan is polishing up glasses and putting them on the shelf. Dewi sits in the corner, already merry after a few pints. Big Nell enters carrying a crate of glasses. As the door opens, 'I Love It' by Icona Pop drifts in from next door.

Big Nell He's playin' that fucking song again, Evan. So help me, if that little wanker doesn't play some new music tonight, I'll have blood on my hands. Week after week the same fucking set. It's our last night, couldn't we hire someone else?

Evan Sorry, Nell my love, Builth and Brecon have dibs on all the best DJs.

Big Nell Those lucky, lucky bastards!

Dewi Builth?! Where? Where are they? We'll show them who's boss, see. No Builthian scum are allowed on these streets! Builth?! Filth!

Evan Pipe down, you, we don't want no trouble.

Dewi Just cos they got the Royal Welsh Show they think they're so special. SCUM! Scum, I tell you!

Evan You rile up the young ones again and I'll cut you off.

Dewi Oop, it's zipped. Not a peep will exit these lips. You have my word; my word now. Word is my bond. Word is my bond, boyo.

Big Nell Don't you think it's time to drop this ridiculous fuckin' feud? It's only a few miles away, you stupid old fuck!

Dewi We have to protect what's ours.

Big Nell What young lad in his right mind is gonna be scared by the likes of you with your big fat gut? You can barely stand up the majority of the time.

Dewi This feud will never die! *Never* while I'm alive on God's green earth will I let those plebeians come into our town and take our women!

Big Nell And what's so wonderful about this place anyway eh? Maybe the women *want* to be taken! Don't they get any choice in the matter?

Evan Now, now. Enough's enough, Nell, don't upset him.

17

Big Nell I'm only sayin' –

Evan I know, love. I know.

Big Nell He's not even from here!

Evan He is now.

Big Nell He's from Merthyr.

Evan Don't let him get under your skin.

Big Nell Why you let him come in here before it's even opening time I'll never know.

Evan Tradition, love – he's been the first at the bar and the last to leave for the last twenty years.

DJ enters in a strop.

DJ I've looked in my dressing room and there's nothing there.

Big Nell I'm sorry?

DJ My rider. I gave it you only last week.

Big Nell Oh, that's right. Sorry, must've misplaced it.

DJ Right, well, I want what was on it as a matter of urgency or I refuse to play.

Big Nell (*deadpan*) Oh no. That would be a crying shame.

Evan What was on it, boy bach?

DJ Don't you boy bach me; I'm no whippersnapper. I want a bottle of Bell's, twenty ciggies and a case of Stella and I want them now.

Evan No probs. I'll bring them over in a tick.

DJ That's more like it.

He leaves.

Big Nell That cunty little shit-face. I can't stand him. Why you let him talk to you that way, Evan?

Evan My hands are tied, love, we need him.

Big Nell Oh please. Any tit can make a Spotify playlist and stick it on week after week; you're paying him for sweet fuck all!

Evan Hush now, love. He'll hear you.

Big Nell So what if he does?! He's a COCK-FACED TWAT!

Evan Christ you've got a mouth on you tonight, 'n you?!

Dewi Time of the month, Nell?

Big Nell What you say to me?!

Dewi (*genuinely afraid*) Nothin'. I said nothin'. I give you my word.

Big Nell That's what I thought.

Evan Right, love, time to open up. The hordes will be here soon.

Big Nell God help us all.

She exits. Evan unlocks the doors.

SCENE FOUR

7.15 p.m. Lights and music fade and we are now inside the chip van. Miv and Mark are cuddled up on the floor, eating chips. Their clothes are on but they are dishevelled. Miv has a serious case of sex hair. They finish the chips.

Mark Mmm, delicious. Right, are you ready for seconds?

Myfanwy Seconds? No, I'm full. I eat too many as it is.

Mark I didn't mean the chips.

Myfanwy Oh.

Mark Once more unto the breach?

Myfanwy You're ready to go again?

Mark What can I say, Miv? You picked a winner.

Myfanwy I'll say.

Mark You drive me wild with desire.

Myfanwy Well, your desire will have to wait; I've got to work.

Mark Fair enough. (*He zips his fly.*)

Myfanwy stands and straightens her clothes. She opens the hatch. Gary is waiting.

Myfanwy Oh hi. Sorry, have you been waiting long?

Gary (*looking at his watch*) You said ten minutes.

Myfanwy Sorry.

Mark (*stands up and sees Gary*) Shit. Hi, Gary. What's up?

Gary Oh hi, Mark . . . What are you, er . . .

Myfanwy He's been helpin' me set up.

Mark That's right. Same time next Friday, Miv? If you need a hand like?

Myfanwy Yeah, same time.

Mark gives her a wink and ducks out the back.

Gary You're fooling no one. You know that, don't you?

Myfanwy It's just a bit of fun.

Gary You can do better.

Myfanwy Have you been waiting around out here this whole time?

Gary In case you needed help.

Myfanwy Perving on me, you mean?

Gary No, I –

Myfanwy Just take your chips and get to fuck!

Gary Sorry, Miv. You know it's only cos I care.

Myfanwy Yeah well, go and care for someone else, alright?

Gary Alright.

Crestfallen he turns to leave, then changes his mind and comes back.

No I can't . . . I want to but I can't . . . I think about you, Myfanwy –

Myfanwy When you're wanking, I know.

Gary No! (*Unable to tell a lie.*) I mean I . . . I do . . . but that's not what I was gonna say.

Myfanwy What were you gonna say?

Gary That you're the first thing I think about when I wake up in the morning –

Myfanwy With an erection.

Gary No! Well yes . . . but that's not what I meant! I think I love you, Miv.

Myfanwy Ah, Gary, that's . . . that's really sweet but it's not love, it's just infatuation. A schoolboy crush.

Gary I'm only three years younger than you!

Myfanwy That's a lot at our age.

Gary I don't think so.

Myfanwy Well, I know so.

Gary Why do you like Mark but you don't like me?

Myfanwy He's sophisticated.

Gary He'd fuck anything that moves.

Myfanwy True. I don't know, I guess I just need a bit of excitement.

Gary What about in a year or two, when I'm eighteen and you're twenty-one?

Myfanwy What about it?

Gary Will you let me take you out then? On a date like?

Myfanwy Don't be ridiculous.

Gary I'm not. I mean it. I'd treat you right, Miv. Roses, chocolates, champagne, the works! Just like you deserve.

Myfanwy You don't even know me. What makes you think I deserve all that?

Gary Because you don't think that you do.

Myfanwy (*smiles*) Yeah, alright then. If I'm still single.

Gary Really?

Myfanwy Really.

Gary Wow.

Myfanwy What?

Gary I'm nervous.

Myfanwy (*laughs*) Well you've got plenty of time to build up your courage.

Gary I better start planning where to take you and that.

Myfanwy I wouldn't decide on a place too soon, it'll probably be shut down by the time we get round to it.

Gary Oh yeah, you're right. Beauty and wisdom: you're the perfect woman.

Myfanwy Alright, now you're startin' to do my head in. Off with you, I got work to do.

Gary Alright . . . sorry . . .

Myfanwy (*good-natured*) No problem, just get to fuck.

Myfanwy turns and gets to work inside the chip van. Jess and Bethan enter. Bethan is heavily pregnant. Jess is already slightly tipsy; she carries a bottle of Tesco own-brand vodka and a protest placard which reads SAVE OUR SCHOOL! *They are both dressed up for a night out, but in cheap Primark clothing.*

Jess It's not cool!

Bethan To close our school! It's not cool!

Jess To close our fuckin' school!

Bethan Alright, cuz?

Gary Oh hi, Bethy.

Jess Lemme hear you say!

Gary / Bethan Fight the power!

Gary Dunno why you're bothered, you hate school.

Jess I do, but it was good for a bunk-off. This political shit's fun, we should go on strike more often.

Bethan I don't want my child's school to be merged with filthy *Builth*.

Jess I'm quite partial to a Builth boy myself.

She mimics the line from the movie Top Gun, *but in a Welsh accent.*

'I got the urge. The urge to merge.'

Bethan What's so special about a Builth boy?

Jess Not much.

Bethan Why then?

Jess I like the thrill of canoodling with the enemy!

Bethan Traitor.

Jess and Bethan laugh.

Jess What you doin' here, Ga? Do Mam and Dad know where you are?

Gary Do Mam and Dad know you're drunk?

Jess Sneak out again, did you? Out the bedroom window is it?

Gary Stealing booze from Dad's secret stash again, are you?

Jess How did you know?

Gary Breath, dum-dum.

Jess Really?

She puts her hand to her mouth and breaths into it and sniffs.

Gary Reprobate! Give us a swig.

Jess Just a quick swill.

Gary Cheers.

She hands him the bottle. He drinks.

Jess Time's up.

Gary Ah come on, Jess, just one more gob full. It's not like Bethy can have any. You'll be a state if you down the lot on your lonesome.

Jess Hmm . . . Let . . . me . . . think. Nah.

Bethan Share the love with your little brother, Jess.

Gary You'll wake in the morning with vomit in your hair.

Jess True. Fight you for it.

Gary Deal.

Jess / Gary One, two, three, four, I declare thumb war. Bow.

They thumb-war. Gary wins and does a lap of honour around the girls.

Gary He shoots, he scores! Hand it over.

Jess grudgingly hands him the bottle. He takes a long swig on it and hands it back.

Jess But you won it?

Gary We were brought up to share. You're the shellfish, not me.

Jess Aw Gary, you sweet little suck-up, what's your game?

Gary No game. Just . . . put in a good word for me, will you.

Bethan With Miv?

Gary Yeah. I'm hopeless. Whenever I'm around her I can barely string a sentence.

Jess Bleuch! Vomiticious!

Bethan Aw, leave him alone! It's sweet. I wish someone loved me like that.

Gary She agreed to go out with me.

Jess Bollocks!

Gary She did! When I'm a bit older.

Bethan How much older.

Gary Two years.

Bethan That's ages!

Gary I can wait.

Jess Gary's in lurrrrve! Gary and Mivvy shagging in a tree S – H – A – G – G – I . . . Oh, doesn't really work, does it?

Gary Shut it, pisshead! You can talk.

Jess I'll shout my love from the hill tops, I don't care who knows.

Gary At least my amour is worthy of my love. Yours is a wet fart in a jam jar.

Jess Hey! Watch it, you!

Gary It's true. He's a big shit-sack full of useless and you know it deep down.

Jess I know no such thing!

Gary Aren't I right, Bethy?

Bethan Umm . . .

Jess Bethan!

Bethan Sorry.

Gary What more proof do you need? Bethan likes everyone.

Jess I know. Stop ganging up on me!

Gary You're a moth ablaze, sissy.

He puts his arm round her and she rests her head on his shoulder.

Jess I know.

Gary Sizzling in the flames.

Jess I know.

Gary Give us a cig.

Bethan (*aghast*) Jess!

Jess I haven't been smoking! My dress is smelly, that's all!

Bethan Jessica!

Jess I gave up! It's been three long hellish days.

Gary Gonads!

Bethan Big hairy ones!

Jess Alright! I had a couple of drags after coitus.

Gary That is disgusting.

Bethan I'm disappointed.

Jess I was weakened! Bathing in the afterglow!

Gary Bleuch! Vomiticious!

Jess Shut up, virgin!

Bethan Jess! Don't be mean.

Gary (*blushing, but summoning all the dignity he can*) Well, Jessica, I don't know what my sexual status has to do with anything, but since you have decided to smear my name in front of our cousin, I shall leave you to your own devices.

He exits.

Jess Ah Gary! Ga! I'm sorry! It just came out. I didn't mean . . . (*He's gone.*) Fuck.

Bethan He'll walk it off.

Jess I'm such a cunt.

She takes a long swig from her bottle. She is clearly a bit drunk now.

Bethan Jess, you know I hate it when you use that word.

Jess It's only a word, Bethan, don't be such a cunt.

Bethan Stop it!

Jess takes an extra long drink, gulping it down. She marches up to the chip van.

Jess Miv! Myfanwy Evans!

Myfanwy Hiya, Jess. Bethan.

Bethan Alright?

Jess My little brother is a prince of the people.

Myfanwy What?

Jess He's a beacon of hope in a mass of mediocrity. I hope you know that. It's important that you do.

Myfanwy If you say so.

Bethan She's right, he is.

Jess Thanks for the back-up, Bethan.

Bethan You're welcome.

Jess You are one lucky lady.

Myfanwy Am I?

Jess (*very serious*) Yes you are. Cos for whatever reason my little brother has chosen you. This golden wonder child has chosen you for his beloved. (*She gets tearful.*) And that boy is a lump of Welsh coal that's turned diamond. So you better appreciate him or you'll have me to answer to. Okay?

Myfanwy Okay. But listen, Jess, Gary and I are not even an item, he's only –

Jess I know that. I know. But treat him gentle, alright?

Myfanwy Alright.

Jess Good. Bethan.

Bethan Yes, Jess?

Jess Let's go.

Bethan Yes, Jess.

They exit into the Pavilion. Mary enters. Myfanwy calls out to her.

Myfanwy Hiya, Mary! Wowzers, look at you all glammed up. London treating you well?

Mary Brilliant. How are you?

Myfanwy Oh, you know . . . same old. Workin' here, workin' at the supermarket, volunteering at the food bank. Scratching by. Just. You hear about the protest?

Mary Yeah. You seen my little sister, she's with my cousin Jess?

Myfanwy Inside.

Mary exits. Myfanwy continues working. Gary reappears and sits looking longingly at the van. Dylan enters.

Dylan How goes it, boy bach?

Gary (*stands respectfully*) Oh hi, Mr Thomas.

Dylan No need for that, lad, we're not in school. Call me Dylan.

Big Nell comes outside for a smoke.

Gary Hi, Dylan. Hi, Nelly.

Big Nell Alright, sweetheart.

Dylan Still pining over Myfanwy?

Gary Yeah.

Dylan She'll come round in the end. Remember what I told you?

Gary 'Perseverance, respect and romance.'

Dylan Good lad.

Big Nell Aw, you fancy Miv, do you?

Gary (*earnest*) I don't fancy her, I love her.

Big Nell Oh, I stand corrected.

Dylan Gary here has been loving her from afar for donkey's. How long is it now Gary?

Gary Two years, four months, three days.

Big Nell It's the afar bit that's holding you back, my lovely. You should get to know her, make her laugh. The way to a woman's heart is through her funny bone. That's how Dyl won mine.

Dylan Listen to the lady. She gives stellar advice.

Gary Thanks. I'll give it my best shot.

Big Nell You coming inside, petal? It's bloody cold out here; you'll catch your death.

Gary No, I think I'll stay out.

Big Nell Suit yourself. I'm going in before my nipples get frostbite and drop off.

Dylan Oh dear God, we can't let that happen! That would be a disaster of epic proportions! Inside! Quick! Quick!

Big Nell exits laughing. Dylan starts to leave.

Gary Mr Thomas.

Dylan Dylan.

Gary Dylan. I'm sorry about what happened like.

Dylan That's alright, Gary.

Gary I think you're a great teacher.

Dylan Thank you, lad. That means a lot. It's only a suspension. I'll be back. For a while anyway.

Gary So what do we do now?

Dylan We wait and we hope for the best.

Gary It was a good turnout though, wasn't it?

Dylan Not bad. Six hundred or thereabouts.

Gary It was exciting. All those people. Teachers, students, parents. I've never been to a protest before.

Dylan May it be the first of many.

Gary Why? You don't think we'll fail, do you? Not with all those signatures.

Dylan We'll see on Monday.

Gary But what will happen then?

Dylan Revolt and rebellion. Who knows?

Gary If you lead a rebellion I'll join.

Dylan You can be my right-hand man. I'll need someone who thinks outside the box.

Gary That'll be me then: 'spaced-out Gary'.

Dylan That's right! The boy with his head in the stars! It's been wonderful to teach someone who's interested in things. You're a good student. Don't let that boring bastard Mr Lewis take that away from you with his adherence to the fuckin' curriculum. Promise me.

Gary He won't. I like history. I'll teach myself . . . until you get back.

Dylan Music to my ears, boy; sweet soul music. I better get inside to her loveliness and give her some adoration. I'll leave you to yours. Stop putting her on a pedestal and start a conversation: you're equals remember.

Gary Okay, I'll do it.

Dylan Good lad. *Viva la revólucion!*

They both hold up their fists. Dylan exits.

SCENE FIVE

8.00 p.m. Cross-fade back to the bar. A group of teenagers enter tentatively.

Teenage Boy Ask him.

Teenage Girl You ask him.

The boy clears his throat and sidles up to the bar with an air of confidence. He puts on the deepest voice he can manage.

Teenage Boy Three pints of your finest ale please, Evan.

Evan OUT! How many times do I have to tell you, we don't serve teenagers in this bar! Go to the pub or buy

32

your alcohol at the offie and drink it before you come in, like everyone else!

They scuttle away. Dylan enters with Big Nell, holding hands.

Dewi Dylan! *Croeso*, Dylan! *Croeso!*

Dylan (*unenthusiastic*) Alright, Dewi.

Dewi And Big Nell! Well I never, the two of you together . . . ? You and Nelly the elephant?!

Big Nell That's right, dickhead.

Dewi How'd it go?!

Dylan You'd know if you'd bothered to turn up. You were a disappointment to me today. You of all people –

Dewi is sheepish.

Dewi Well, I would have been there like . . . it's just . . .

Dylan Evan and Nell were there. Why weren't you?

Dewi I'm a bit old for that now, Dylan. I don't have the stamina I used to. I was there in spirit, that's the point.

Dylan Is it?

Evan The usual, Dylan?

Dylan That's right, plus one for yourself and one for the lovely lady.

Evan Haven't seen you here in a while.

Dylan Everyone will be here for the last disco, I couldn't miss that!

Big Nell Let me get these, Dyl.

Dylan No, no, you two are losing your jobs. I'll get them.

Big Nell 'No I will. Dylan got suspended from work on Monday.

Dylan We're all three of us in a fine mess.

Dewi What's this? I never heard about this.

Dylan The headmistress says I'm politicising the children.

Evan But the whole town was behind you, mun.

Dylan She says party politics have no place in the classroom, but if I can't teach the children the history of their own country, then what's the point in being a teacher?

Big Nell No point.

Dylan She accused me of being the ringleader of the children's strike.

Evan Were you?

Dylan I went through the proper avenues and contacted our union to arrange a strike as is my right. If the students want to join in, who am I to stop them?

Big Nell She's doesn't give a toss about the kids, she's angling to be the headmistress of two schools instead of one.

Dewi That grotty, shitty little Tory-loving fuck!

Dylan Enough. We're here for a night out. Let's make it one to remember, shall we?!

Evan Absolutely. This round's on me.

Dewi You're a saint, Evan! A saint, I tell you!

Big Nell I'm goin' for a slash. (*Flirtatiously to Dylan.*) Don't you dare stare at my arse as I walk away.

She goes. None of the men can tear their eyes away.

Dewi Fuckin' hell, Dylan, how long has this been goin' on, mun?!

Dylan Mind your own.

Dewi Oh come on, Dylan, you can't stay mad at me for ever.

Dylan Can't I?

Dewi Tell us some of the juicy details. I have to live vicarious.

Dylan A gentleman never tells.

Dewi She's *gigantic*! I don't think I could cope.

Dylan The more fool you: gutless wonder that you are. She's everything you could wish for in a woman.

Dewi Not that I haven't thought about it, mind . . .

Evan Oh, here we go.

Dylan and Evan look on amused as Dewi disappears into fantasy.

Dewi Vast buttocks: round and ready, springy and spongey; like a bouncy castle ready to be jumped on. Bosoms that could smother you into a delightful death. Great curves like the rolling hills of Powys and Carmarthenshire. I tell you: I could disappear into her peaks and valleys and never come up for air. What a woman! What a mountain of fleshy goodness. Every man should experience the love of a woman like that, at least once. Go on, Dylan, throw us a bone.

Dylan Dynamite, I tell you, dynamite! I can now die: happy as a shitty pig.

Dewi is saucer-eyed. Big Nell re-enters.

Big Nell Iechyd da! (*She downs her drink in one.*)

Dewi can't stop staring.

You okay there, Dewi?

Dewi What? Oh why, yes, thank you, Nelly, and how are you this fine evening?

Big Nell Dylan, what shit has Dewi been makin' up about me now?

Dylan Only an ode to your loveliness, my precious one.

He kisses her.

Big Nell Aww, come over here and sit with me in the shadows. Let's have a *cwtch*.

Dylan With pleasure, my sweet. Do you want to stare into each other's eyes or would you prefer a cheeky fondle under the table?

Big Nell Whatever takes your fancy.

Music and lights. A blast of 'Single Ladies' by Beyoncé. Jess, Bethan and Mary dance into the next scene.

SCENE SIX

9.00 p.m. The women's toilets. The night is now in full swing. Jess is drunk and crying in a heap on the floor; Mary and Bethan are comforting her.

Jess But I loves him . . .

Bethan I know, Jess, I know.

Jess I just loves him so much.

Bethan I know you do.

Jess I really, really –

Bethan Loves him. Believe me, I know.

Mary It's disgusting.

Jess He's gorgeous and handsome and gorgeous!

36

Bethan I know he is.

Mary Don't encourage her, Bethan.

Jess And he loves me!

Mary I doubt that somehow.

Jess He does! He told me.

Bethan What else did he tell you?

Jess He said: 'Jessica, light of my life, fire of my loins. My sin, my soul.'

Bethan Aw, really? That's poetry that is.

Mary He nicked it.

Jess What?

Mary It's from *Lolita*, and a pretty apt reference as it happens.

Jess Alright, smart-arse. We can't all be literature experts like you.

Mary For all the good it's done me.

Jess He makes me feel special.

Mary He's made half the female population of this town feel special.

Bethan Jess . . . Don't forget Mary and him . . .

Jess Oh sorry, Mary, I forgot.

Mary It's fine, it was a decade ago.

Jess He said he'd rescue me from this fuckin' place.

Bethan Oh shit.

Jess What?

Bethan He said the same thing to Anne-Marie.

Jess Anne-Marie Price?!

Bethan Yeah.

Jess When?!

Bethan (*trying to placate her*) Oh ages ago, way before you and him, Jess.

Jess Before me?!

Bethan Yeah, it was at least two weeks ago.

Mary Jessica, he's a bastard. Get rid of him; he's got kids all over. If you want to get out of here, do it! Don't rely on any fucking man to do it for you. Do yourself a favour and get rid, before you're up the duff like Bethan and stuck here forever!

Bethan Oh cheers, sis.

Jess That wanker! I'll kill him!

Mary Sorry, Beth, I didn't mean it.

Bethan Yes you did.

Jess I'll rip him to shreds!

Bethan Calm down.

Jess Calm down?! I loves him! I'm gonna gut him like a fuckin' fish!

Jess storms out, closely followed by Bethan and Mary.

Mary Jess! Jess, he's not worth it!

SCENE SEVEN

9.05 p.m. Lloyd is sitting on a wall outside the chip van eating chips. Mark approaches.

Mark Alright, Lloyd?

Lloyd Windy! What girl's skirt you been sniffing up tonight?

Mark Myfanwy's, as it happens.

Lloyd Fuck, man, how do you do it?

Mark Well, aside from my devastating good looks, I got charm and charisma coming out the old wazoo. I learned it in books, see. Read a few books, Lloyd, and you'll have them eating out the palm of your hand.

Lloyd Books? What like? *Twilight* and that *Shades of Grey* shite?

Mark Nah, not that bollocks, I'm talking about the greats: Shakespeare, Nabokov, Austen, stuff you can sink your teeth into! Stuff you can quote to impress or rip off without them knowing about it. The more you read, the more you'll fuck. Trust me, their knickers will be round their ankles in no time. Never fails, Lloyd. Never fails.

Lloyd You're a dirty dog, mun.

Mark You knows it.

Jess (*from offstage*) I will tear your fuckin' face off!

Mark Uh-oh.

Jess enters in a fury and launches herself at Mark's face, scratching and biting. Mary and Bethan run in behind her. Lloyd pulls her off and holds her back.

Jessica, light of my life! Fire of my –

Jess You fuckin' fraud! Did you think I wouldn't work it out? You think I'm stupid, do you?!

Mark Jessica, as if I could ever think that! It hurts me you could ever accuse me of such a notion! You are my –

Jess Your what?! Your floozy? Your strumpet? Your Lolita?

Mark I was going to say beloved! And believe me, it pains me to hear you speak of yourself in such terms. It cuts me to the quick, Jessica. It sears me to the bone. So high is my regard for you, I can hardly bear it.

Jess Oh shut up, Windy! Whoever gave you that nickname was spot on. Brimful of hot air!

Mark Jessica!

Jess How many others are there?

Myfanwy What's this about, Mark?

Jess Oh, don't tell me. He's been in you too, has he?

Myfanwy Jess, I had no idea, honestly . . . I would never –

Mark I can explain, Jess –

Jess Don't bother!

She takes off her stiletto shoe and threatens him with it.

If you ever come near me again, I'll stiletto you in the face. Got it?

Mark nods, genuinely afraid. Jess hobbles off, still holding one shoe in her hand. Bethan follows her. Lloyd is pissing himself laughing.

Bethan Jess! Jess, wait up!

Myfanwy Oh shit. Jess! I'm sorry!

Lloyd That was fuckin' class, man! Hilarious!

He goes inside. Myfanwy goes back to serving chips. Mary approaches Mark.

Mary Mark.

Mark is stunned to see her. He drops his Lothario act and speaks from the heart.

Mark Mary.

Mary Oh, you remember?

Mark Of course I remember.

Mary I would've thought there'd been so many by now that we all blur into one. No?

Mark Not when it comes to you, Mary. I could never forget you.

Mary I wish I could forget.

Mark Don't say that.

Mary Why not? It's true.

Mark What are you doin' here?

Mary Visiting my family.

Mark It's been a while.

Mary Yeah, well, my little sister is pregnant and about to pop, and my mam is going nuts, so . . .

Mark Right . . . Yeah.

Mary Someone's gotta look out for her.

Mark Of course.

Mary She's sixteen years old.

Mark I know.

Mary You like 'em young, don't you?

Mark I don't know what you think, but I never –

Mary She won't tell us who. Says she doesn't know; pretends she's put it around a bit to throw us off the scent. But I know. I can smell you all over her.

Mark I never touched her, Mary.

Mary I begged her to get rid of it but she refused.

Mark I swear on my life. I would never, not her.

Mary Stay away from her. I mean it.

She exits. He goes to Myfanwy in her chip van.

Mark Miv –

Myfanwy Get to fuck, Windy, alright?

Mark Yeah, alright.

He exits. Gary appears out of the shadows.

Gary Hate to say I told you so.

Myfanwy I don't need protecting. Go home.

Gary I don't like to see you hurt.

Myfanwy I'm not, believe me. I could give two shits about that idiot.

Gary Then why –

Myfanwy Cos I felt like it, alright?! I'm not some virginal delicate flower that needs a sixteen-year-old boy to look out for her. I can look after myself!

Gary (*blurts out*) Knock, knock.

Myfanwy What?

Gary It's a joke. Knock, knock.

Myfanwy (*perplexed but playing along*) Who's there?

Gary Europe.

Myfanwy Europe who?

Gary No, you're a poo!

He laughs hard. Myfanwy laughs too, but more at him than at the joke.

Serious, though what do you want to be when you grow up?

Myfanwy What?

Gary Your plans for the future, what are they?

Myfanwy I am grown-up. I don't have any.

Gary Are you happy working in the chip van?

Myfanwy It's work.

Gary I used to want to be an astronaut.

Myfanwy Oh?

Gary Now I think . . . that's stupid . . . A bit naive like.

Myfanwy How do you become one of them?

Gary I'd need a degree: maths, science or engineering. My parents are skint so I can forget about that. I asked the careers advisor at school, she told me to set my sights a bit lower; keep my feet on the ground: the army maybe.

Myfanwy The army?

Gary If I learn to be a pilot then I might be able to apply but it's still unlikely cos we don't have a space programme. But at least I'd get to travel. Learn new skills.

Myfanwy What kind of careers advisor tells a boy to join the army?

Gary There aren't any Welsh astronauts.

Myfanwy Why not?

Gary You need dual nationality. John Llewellyn could have been one of the first men on the moon, but he never made it into space because he failed to pilot a jet aircraft

43

blindfolded. Now there's Dafydd Rhys Williams, but he's Canadian really, he wasn't born or raised here, so he doesn't count either.

Myfanwy You sound like an expert.

Gary Outer space is my favourite.

Myfanwy Why an astronaut?

Gary It would be incredible, don't you think? To be up there above the clouds, in the dark looking down on the world and all its countries and oceans. Imagining all the lives being lived out below me. Watching the earth like a bright blue marble, lit from within, shining and rolling around in the night.

Myfanwy Floating from room to room.

Gary Yeah, it'd be like flying or swimming slowly through the air.

Myfanwy Sucking food through a straw. Would the stars seem closer when you were up there, do you think?

Gary No, they'd still be too far away. Each star is a sun you see, some with their own planets orbiting around them and some of those with life too, I reckon.

Myfanwy Wow. Really?

Gary Must be. It's too vast for us to be the only ones. We are not alone, Miv. It's not possible.

Myfanwy I wonder what Wales looks like from space?

Gary Tiny. A minuscule little pin-prick of a country.

Myfanwy S'pose so.

Gary Sometimes when I really think long and hard about the universe and our planet and human existence, it hurts my brain.

Myfanwy You think about all that a lot, do you?

Gary Of course! Don't you?

Myfanwy No. It gives me a sinking feeling. I try not to.

Gary Oh.

Myfanwy I'm not very clever.

Gary That's not true.

Myfanwy How would you know?

Gary What did you want to be when you saw the careers advisor?

Myfanwy Oh . . . uh . . . a singer or an actress.

Gary What did she tell you?

Myfanwy She said they were tough professions and that I should probably concentrate on working towards more realistic goals where there would be more opportunity for employment.

Gary So what subjects did you take for A-levels?

Myfanwy Maths and Business Studies. I failed.

Gary That doesn't mean you're not clever. It just means you're no good at exams. Everyone's got strengths and weaknesses. 'Trust that you will have your own shining moment and maintain an enquiring mind.'

Myfanwy Where did you get that from?

Gary Mr Thomas. He's my favourite teacher.

Myfanwy Yeah, I liked him too.

Gary That careers advisor, she's full of shit, you could be an actress, a singer, or both if you want to.

Myfanwy Do you think?

Gary I know it in my bones.

Myfanwy How?

Gary You've got the X-factor!

Myfanwy Thanks. You could be an astronaut too I reckon.

Gary Nah. It's pie in the sky. The army is the only way out of here for me.

Myfanwy Don't join the army, Gary.

Gary Why not?

Myfanwy You'd have to kill people. That's not you.

Gary I could do it if I had to. Fight for my country.

Myfanwy You could get hurt or killed.

Gary You care about me, Myfanwy?

Myfanwy Of course I do.

Gary (*grins*) I knew it.

Myfanwy I didn't mean it like that.

Gary You don't want to lose me. Never fear, my sweet, I shall not leave your side even for an instant. We shall be together for always!

Myfanwy (*laughing*) Listen to you! You've been taking tips from Windy?

Gary Never! Well maybe a little bit . . . but you liked it, so . . .

Myfanwy Don't talk like him, it doesn't suit you.

Gary Okay.

    Pause.

Myfanwy Sometimes . . . I wish I was young again.

Gary You are young.

Myfanwy No, I mean back when I was really tiny.

Gary Why?

Myfanwy It was lovely being a kiddywink, don't you think? Worry free. Just playing in the mud and paddling in the stream.

Gary Making dens in the trees.

Myfanwy Chasing butterflies.

Gary Collecting stickers.

Myfanwy Wales was beautiful to me back then. Everything was simple when you were looked after by your mammy. There were no exams to fail. No money worries, no future plans and every story had a happy ending.

Gary No heartbreak.

Myfanwy No chips to serve to drunken idiots! No handing out food at the food bank to people with hungry bellies and empty hopeless eyes! Why does life have to be so hard?

Gary I don't know, Myfanwy.

Myfanwy Oh, take me back there. Let me be a little girl again.

Gary We can't though, can we?

Myfanwy No.

Gary We could go paddling, though. Have a splash and a play. Lighten the load; brighten the spirit.

Myfanwy In the summer sun.

Gary Blissful.

Myfanwy I'd love that.

Gary It's a date. Any time you wanna go, just say the word.

Myfanwy I will. Hey, I got an idea.

Gary Yeah?

Myfanwy You wanna come serve chips tonight? Danny didn't show up for his shift.

Gary Yes, please!

Myfanwy I'll make sure you're paid.

Gary Thanks, Miv.

Myfanwy No need, I could use the help.

Gary I've never had a job before, only work experience.

Myfanwy Well, it's not as exciting as space travel but it's a start.

Gary I can put it on my CV! My first job!

Myfanwy (*laughs*) Yes, I suppose you can.

Gary The chippy: the first rung on the professional ladder to success.

They laugh.

SCENE EIGHT

Music and lights. The music dips and a light illuminates Big Nell. She addresses the audience. The cast enact what she's describing.

Big Nell It's ten p.m. and everyone is well away! This . . . is the bewitching hour. The pressure is on. The animals have zoned in on their targets and they're almost inebriated

48

enough to woo themselves a lover for the evening's shenanigans.

They eye one another provocatively from across the room, baring their teeth and licking their lips. The girls flutter their eyelashes and flick at their hair, pretending not to notice the not-so-subtle glances in their direction.

But here we go: one of the boys is taking the plunge and the rest of the pack will soon follow. Doing his best to hide the panic in his eyes and the lurch in his guts, and the tingle in his testicles; he struts, confident as a peacock, across the dance floor and gatecrashes the conversation. But wait! Oh dear, the music is so loud that they must stand unnaturally close to one another in order to hear. Shame.

The girl laughs too loud at jokes that aren't funny, and throws back her head dramatically, exposing her kissable neck. Emboldened by this response he moves a little closer. She can feel . . . and smell, his beautiful beer breath on her face. They lock eyes. He smirks. She giggles. And convinced he's some kind of irresistible, comic genius he moves in for the kill!

They snog each other's faces off.
Blackout.

SCENE NINE

10.00 p.m. Back in the bar. Jess and Bethan are sitting at a table drinking. Jess surreptitiously adds vodka to her drink from a hip-flask. Bethan drinks orange juice. Mary sits with them sipping a G and T. Lloyd and Will are at the bar. Dewi is playing darts drunkenly on his own.

Lloyd Hey, Will, watch this. Doubles all round, Nelly, you sexy bitch.

Lloyd and Will laugh.

49

Big Nell No offence, Lloyd, but I'd rather vomit blood.

Will Fuckin' hell, Nell, that's a bit dark.

Lloyd Yeah, no need for that, Nell, I was only joking.

Will Don't be hurt, Lloyd, it's just she's in love with me. Ain't that right, Nell?

Big Nell Yeah, I can hardly contain myself. After one night with Willy Jenkins, no other man will do.

Will When are you going to ditch Dylan and run away with me?

Big Nell When this town reaches one hundred per cent employment.

Evan Enough, boys. Stop harassing my staff.

Mary gets up to go to the loo.

Lloyd Look at the arse on that one over there.

Will Fuck me, I'd like to give her one.

Lloyd (*to Mary*) Alright, beautiful, my friend likes you.

Mary Oh yeah, I bet he does. Likes me for my personality does he?

She exits.

Lloyd With a rack like that, who cares about personality?

Jess You're wasting your time, boys. Mary's graduated from university, she's got a job in London, she's not interested in the likes of you.

Will Oh, hoity-toity posh bitch now, is she?

Lloyd Too good for us, is that it?

Bethan She is, as a matter of fact.

Will (*to Jess*) What about you then. You'll do.

Jess Well, that's very romantic, but I think I'll pass.

Lloyd Why's that then?

Jess Are we supposed to be grateful to you for objectifying us?

Lloyd Eh?

Jess Am I supposed to enjoy being treated like a walking fuck-hole?

Lloyd and Will laugh at this.

Will You said it, love, not me.

Lloyd Looks like we're wasting our time on her, Will, but this one's preggers, so she's obviously up for it. What do you say, darlin'?

Will I'm told she says 'YES! YES! YES!'

Jess Piss off, will you? Don't listen to them, Beth.

Bethan It's alright, Jess.

Lloyd Fuckin' hell, love, how old are you? Babies popping out babies.

Evan Boys, that's enough.

Will I heard she's a real goer.

Lloyd Nice big milky tits. I'd still give her one.

Jess You shut your fucking mouth!

Lloyd Little slut, bet she'd love it.

Evan Boys, enough I said.

Will Takes after her mother then, does she?

Lloyd That's right. Where's your mum? She's always gagging for it.

Bethan runs out sobbing.

Jess Dickheads. Beth!

Jess exits after her.

Big Nell That's it! Out, the pair of you!

Lloyd Oh come on, Nelly, we're only joking around.

Big Nell Yeah, well, it's not funny. That girl has enough to deal with, without the likes of you picking her apart for your own amusement.

Evan She's right, boys, leave off her or you'll be barred next time.

Big Nell Next time?! There is no next time!

Evan Oh yeah, I forgot.

Big Nell Well then?

Evan Boys will be boys.

Big Nell Fuck's sake, Evan!

Evan What?

Dewi Bullseye!

Big Nell Bullseye?! You didn't even hit the board!

Dewi I am the champion. I am the champion! No time for losers cos I am the champion!

Dewi takes dangerous aim and throws another dart which knocks a pint glass off the bar. It smashes.

Big Nell That's it! No more darts for you.

Dewi Aww. Please, Nell. I'll be careful.

Big Nell Any other bar you'd be out on your ear. Give them to me, Dewi! Give them here!

She tries to confiscate the darts but Dewi runs around like a drunken schoolboy, giggling.

During this Catrin enters. She wears a business suit that is out of place amongst the rest of crowd. The noise in the bar dulls when they see her.

Catrin I'm looking for Dylan. Is he here?

Big Nell and Dewi notice her and immediately stop what they're doing. They speak simultaneously.

Big Nell / No.

Dewi / Yeah.

Big Nell (*warning in her voice*) Dewi.

Dewi Haven't seen him.

Catrin I was told he was here.

No one responds.

Fine, I'll wait. Do you have a wine list?

A faint sniggering can be heard from around the bar. Big Nell ignores her completely.

Excuse me?

Big Nell looks straight at her but does not move.

Your barmaid is refusing to serve me. Evan.

Evan I'm terribly sorry. What would you like, Catrin? Nell, get Catrin a drink.

Dewi Booo! Hisss!

Big Nell I refuse to serve a woman who asks for a fuckin' wine list in the Pivvy.

Catrin I'll take a gin and tonic then.

Big Nell You're under-age.

Catrin I'm thirty-four.

Evan Nell, make the woman a drink.

Big Nell Oh Evan, when will you grow a backbone?!

Evan I'm doing my job.

Big Nell She's too young to be a head teacher. You got the job cos you went to Oxford. They should have promoted Dylan.

Catrin They wanted someone looking to the future, not backwards.

Dewi They wanted a boot-licker!

Catrin I'm here to talk to Dylan. Not the entire town.

Big Nell How are your best mates at the council?

Catrin This has nothing to do with you.

Big Nell You should be supporting your staff. Instead you suck up to councillors to secure your own fat pay cheque at the end of it all.

Dewi Boooo!

Catrin I don't get paid as much as you seem to think, I can assure you. I am not the enemy here.

Big Nell Yes, you are.

Catrin I see, and may I ask why that would be?

Big Nell How about the suspension of one of the hardest working teachers in your school?

Catrin The children have been on strike all week, he left me no choice.

Dylan enters.

Dylan Hello, Catrin.

Catrin You didn't show up for our meeting. I've been calling you all day.

Dylan I was busy.

Catrin I need a private word. It won't take long.

Dylan Whatever you have to say, you can say it right here.

Catrin Have it your way. Call the protests off, Dylan. It doesn't help your case.

Dylan I disagree.

Catrin You're putting me in an impossible position.

Dylan It's not your position I'm worried about, I'm thinkin' about my students.

Catrin Wales has had over fifteen years of devolution but our test scores are behind, both the schools are in special measures –

Dylan Falling behind, are we? With cuts, school closures, compulsory redundancies, bigger classes? Really?

Catrin That's the same across the whole of Britain.

Dylan What use is devolution when there isn't any money?

Catrin One school operating across two sites will improve standards. Mergers lead to economies of scale, we can provide a full curriculum –

Dylan How much? What's the saving?

Catrin A hundred and twenty thousand a year.

Dylan Sack a couple of people at the council. Make the saving that way.

Catrin That offer's not on the table.

Dylan turns his back; he is breathing heavily and suddenly looks very tired.

Big Nell Get out.

Evan Nell.

Big Nell You shouted yourself hoarse at the protest this morning but faced with her in the bar you smile and whimper, bow and scrape. Well, that's up to you, but I won't do it. I will not serve that woman a drink. Not now. Not ever.

Dewi You tell her, Nell!

Catrin We're doing the best we can under the circum-stances; it's a thankless task I can tell you that! The whole town ready to latch on to your throat when all I want is to find a solution. But if you all think I'm going to be intimidated into hiding you are mistaken. The children must return to school. They listen to you. Call off the strike.

Dylan That's not up to me.

Catrin Haven't you embarrassed me enough?!

Nell explodes.

Big Nell Get out of here, you milkless tit!

Catrin leaves the bar furiously, slamming the door behind her. 'I Love It' by Icona Pop comes on again.

Arrrrrgh! This fucking song *again*! There will be blood!

She exits to the dance hall. Evan follows her.

Evan No, Nell! Don't! We need him, love!

Nell storms into the dance hall. Loud music is playing and men and women are dancing in single-sex groups;

glancing over at one another every now and then. Nell gets up on to the platform with the DJ and they shout at one another over the music. Evan tries to placate them. Nell pushes past the DJ and stops the music. The men and women protest.

DJ What do you think you're doing?

Big Nell Pick something else quick before we have a mutiny on our hands.

DJ Apologies, folks. Just a minor glitch in the system.

Big Nell I'll glitch your fucking system if you play that song one more time!

The DJ puts on 'Come On Eileen' by Dexys Midnight Runners. The dancers cheer.

There, was that so hard?!

Big Nell exits back into the bar, closely followed by the DJ and Evan, arguing as they go.

DJ I cannot work under these conditions, Evan!

Evan I'm terribly sorry, boyo, it won't happen again.

DJ Nobody has permission to touch my equipment but me.

Big Nell Equipment?! An iPad and a fucking jack lead!

DJ I am an artist, I have music in my veins.

Big Nell Oh I beg your pardon, what instrument do you play? Are you a singer? Hum us a tune then, sing us an aria!

DJ Evan I will not put up with this treatment any longer. I'll let this one pass cos I'm a professional but any more interference and I'm terminating my set.

He stomps off.

Evan Now you've done it.

Big Nell Oh come on, Evan, what difference can it possibly make now?!

Evan Nell! Not tonight! It's the last one, try to enjoy it, will you?

Dylan Come on, Nell, let's go have a dance, eh?

Big Nell Alright.

Dylan Get out there, you sexy beast! Show them how it's done!

Dylan slaps Big Nell's arse and they dance out of the bar into the hall. Another blast of 'Come On Eileen'; the cast sing along and dance into the next scene.

SCENE TEN

Bethan is on the floor of the toilets with her back against the wall crying. The girls sit on either side of her; Mary holds her hand and Jess rests her head on Bethan's stomach. They sing the Welsh lullaby 'Ar Hyd y Nos' ('All through the Night') to her pregnant belly. Gradually the rest of the cast begin to join in and surround her. Bethan stops crying. At some point the lullaby turns into a hum and Bethan speaks her monologue over the top of this.

Jess / Mary
Holl amrantau'r sêr ddywedant
Ar hyd y nos
'Dyma'r ffordd i fro gogoniant,'
Ar hyd y nos.
Golau arall yw tywyllwch
I arddangos gwir brydferthwch
Teulu'r nefoedd mewn tawelwch
Ar hyd y nos.

O mor siriol, gwena seren
Ar hyd y nos
I oleuo'i chwaer ddaearen
Ar hyd y nos.
Nos yw henaint pan ddaw cystudd
Ond i harddu dyn a'i hwyrddydd
Rhown ein golau gwan i'n gilydd
Ar hyd y nos.

Bethan They can talk all they want. I know they do. I know the names they call me . . . what they think of me. But I know. I know I will love my baby more than they will ever love anything. And when my girly girl or my boy bach is born it will burst out of me on a wave of loveliness. No one can take that away cos my love is real. It is happiness that is growing inside me; love that is swelling up my belly big and round like the globe. And my baby will *be* my whole world. My little he or she will be all that I need on this planet. My little life is plenty big enough for me, for us. My baby is mine and only mine and I won't be alone any more.

Jess suddenly shoots to the other end of the room. The rest of the cast, except for the three girls, scatter.

Jess Whoa! Holy shitting hell, it moved!

Bethan It does that sometimes.

Jess It kicked me in the face!

Bethan and Mary are in stitches.

Mary Doesn't like your singing voice, obviously.

Bethan It's moving around loads now.

Mary Aw, can I feel?

Bethan Knock yourself out.

She places Mary's hands on her belly.

59

Mary Oh my God! That's amazing.

Jess comes over again and tentatively touches Bethan's belly, then shoots off to the other end of the room again.

Jess (*jumping up and down*) Aaah! It's freaking me out! I don't like it! It's like there's an alien in there!

Bethan Thanks!

Jess Sorry, it's just so weird!

Mary It's amazing, Bethan. You're amazing.

Bethan (*smiles*) I know.

Jess I am *never* having one of those! I am *never* having children!

Bethan It's alright, you get used to it.

Jess *Never.*

Mary You don't have to have one if you don't want to.

Jess *Good.*

Bethan What will you do instead?

Jess I dunno, but from now on I'm goin' on the pill, and getting a coil and I'm gonna use a diaphragm *and* a condom all at once!

Bethan (*laughing*) You're hilarious, Jess.

Jess I mean it! Men have it so easy. If all I had to do was squirt out a couple of pumps of gizz to have a kid it would be one thing. I mean they do that every morning, wanking in the shower! But to have to grow it inside me for nine months, push it out and feed it; ruining my body in the process, and then insult of all insults give it *his* family name! Fuckin' forget about it. I refuse!

Mary You could give it your name if you wanted to.

Jess Come on, Mary; what man do you know who would agree to that? Self-important arseholes the lot of them.

Bethan Gary would.

Jess My brother is not a man. He's an angel sent down from heaven to make me look bad.

Mary So it's a feminist stand you're taking?

Jess Yes! That and I don't like babies.

Bethan Aww, why not?!

Jess They're ugly.

Bethan They're not!

Jess Squishy pink faces like little old men.

Bethan Only at first, they get cuter.

Jess They give me the creeps.

Bethan Why?!

Jess The way they stare at you for ages and ages. They're a bit intense. Puts me on edge. They need to lighten up. Creepy little creatures.

Mary and Bethan laugh.

Bethan What about you, Mary? Do you want kids?

Mary Maybe one day. I couldn't do it on my own though. You're so brave, Beth.

Bethan Not really. I'm quite scared actually.

Mary Of what?

Bethan The birth bit. I don't want to be on my own for the birth bit.

Mary Won't Mam be with you?

Bethan No. She's so angry at me; I don't want her there.

Mary Jess'll go with you.

Jess NO! NO FUCKING WAY! Sorry, Beth, but no.

Bethan Would you come in with me, Mary?

Mary Me?

Bethan To hold my hand? I'm frightened. You're stronger than anyone else I know. I think you're the only person who'll be able to cope with it.

Mary Cope with what?

Bethan I've heard rumours . . .

Mary What?

Bethan Apparently you shit the bed.

Jess Jesus fucking Christ!

Bethan I know! I'll be mortified, Mary!

Mary (*laughing*) You'll be fine!

Bethan I'll die of shame!

Mary The midwife sees women shit the bed every day.

Jess (*dry retches*) Can we please change the subject? (*Dry retches again.*)

Bethan Will you come with me?

Mary Of course I will. It will be an honour. I can't wait to see your beautiful baby . . . (*Starts to giggle.*) All covered in shit.

Mary and Bethan collapse into laughter. Jess dry retches into the sink.

SCENE ELEVEN

Back in the bar everyone is pissed as a fart. Dylan and Big Nell are snogging in the corner. Dewi is singing the Welsh National Anthem drunkenly and out of tune. No one else is singing.

Dewi (*chorus*)
  Gwlad, Gwlad, pleidiol wyf i'm gwlad –

(*To Lloyd and Will.*) Join in, lads, come on!

  *Tra môr yn fur i'r bur hoff bau,
  O bydded i'r heniaith barhau.*

Why you not join in, lads? It does the heart good to sing.

Lloyd We don't know the words.

Dylan What?

Lloyd Never learnt them.

Big Nell But you learn Welsh at school.

Will Not really.

Big Nell What words do you know?

Will *Pysgod y schlodion* – fish and chips. *Bore da* – hello.

Big Nell *Shwmae.*

Will What?

Big Nell Hello.

Will Huh?

Big Nell Never mind.

Will *Dym ysmgu yschwelchynda* – no smoking please. Oh, and I can count to twenty.

Dylan Do you know what the words to the anthem mean at least?

Will No.

Lloyd No, and we don't want to.

Dylan This land of my fathers is dear to me –

Lloyd I said we don't wanna know.

Dylan
Land of poets and singers, and people of stature
Her brave warriors, fine patriots
Shed their blood for freedom.

Lloyd We're not listening!

Dylan
Land! Land! I am true to my land!
As long as the sea serves as a wall for this pure, dear land
May the language endure forever –

Lloyd I said save your breath!

Will I'm not into poetry.

Dylan Well, that may well be, but the sentiment surely?

Lloyd You don't half go on! Blah fuckin' blah. You're not our teacher any more, leave us alone.

Big Nell Forget it, Dyl, it's pointless.

Lloyd Right, whose round is it!

Will Yours.

Dewi Make mine a double, Lloyd.

Lloyd We're not even drinkin' with you, you cheeky old fuck.

Evan Play nice, boys. He's drunk, he doesn't know what he's sayin'.

Dewi Come on, boys, you owe me one from last week.

Dylan stands. His voice booms from across the room. The bar goes silent.

Buy the man a drink, pipsqueak!

Lloyd Why should I?

Dylan Cos he deserves it and you don't, that's why! He worked down the mines in his day. He's been down into the bowels of the earth and held this country's black guts in his hands! What have you ever done?!

Lloyd I done enough . . . (*Mutters under his breath.*) And you're not my teacher any more, old man.

Dylan What? What did you say? (*Pause.*) Answer me, boy!

Lloyd I said I done enough.

Dylan Enough? Enough?! Have you had your livelihood snatched away from you after years of backbreaking labour? Have you stood in picket lines day after day, fighting for your right to work?!

Lloyd There aren't any jobs to fight for.

Dylan That's right, there aren't any. You go and stand in the dole queue every other week, Lloyd, but have you ever stopped to question why?

Lloyd Mining has got fuck all to do with anything. This wasn't even a mining town, so why the fuck do you go on about it all the fuckin' time?!

Dylan Everything within our history leads us to the present day, Lloyd. No man stands alone.

Lloyd Yeah, yeah. I've heard it all before, I been in your history lessons.

Will Weren't you just sacked for not sticking to the curriculum, Dyl?

Dylan Suspended, not sacked! I dunno, you have a fart at one end of this town and by the time you get to the other, the rumour is you shat yourself. Suspended, boy, and it was a black day, I can tell you. A black, black day.

Dewi is slurring drunk and not really following the conversation, just picking out bits of information.

Dewi Black, black days. I protest! We protested the loss of our jobs.

Dylan I know you did, Dewi.

Dewi (*cries*) We tried.

Dylan I know.

Dewi (*drunkenly mumbled*) My first day.

Dylan What's that, Dew?

A box of light opens on the floor surrounding Dewi. As he stands and tells his story the other men in the cast surround him as if they are miners standing in a lift. They switch their helmet lights on. Dylan takes on the role of Dewi's father.

Dewi My first day. Sixteen years old and shaking in my boots, which were two sizes too big for me, cos they'd belonged to my eldest brother Sam, who'd been buried only a month before. Crushed when a tunnel collapsed in on him.

The sound of the lift descending.

My heart was beating so hard, I thought it would hop right out of my mouth and bounce along the floor. A group of men packed together like animals in a cage descending through the earth's gaping jaws and down into the throat of the world.

Dewi reaches for Dylan's hand.

I grabbed at my father's hand and he shoved it away, embarrassed. We juddered to a halt and climbed out into an indescribable blackness.

The lift judders and stops and the men climb out and disperse. Dewi stays in the box of light, afraid.

You've never been in the dark till you've been down deep into the earth like that; it has a treacle thickness to it . . . like it's ready to consume you. I was afraid if the lamps went out, it would spirit me away never to be seen again. So many boys went down and never came back out. It was the ultimate fear: becoming one of the disappeared. I still have nightmares.

The smell of the dust . . . coal dust heavy in the air . . . that was the stench of the treacle dark we breathed in day after day . . . breathing in the blackness and the darkness that was slowly smothering us and coughing it up again. Every man in the family had black heaving coughs, black phlegm, and black lungs. Our father died of it and our mother placed lumps of coal over his eyes.

The lights snap back up. Dewi, a drunken wreck of a man, is babbling nonsense and crying into his pint.

Lloyd Well, fuck that. You wouldn't catch me working down there.

Will There's some more jobs at Tesco opening up soon, the job centre have set up interviews.

Big Nell Tesco? Tesco has shut down every other shop in this town.

Will We need the work, Nell.

Big Nell If it's jobs you're looking for there's some care work going.

Lloyd I'm not wiping decrepit shitty arses for a living.

Will What's the pay?

Big Nell Same as Tesco. Minimum wage.

Lloyd Forget it. We're better off living at home.

Evan (*as he lays out a round of drinks*) Your drinks, boys. Dylan, Dewi, these are on me.

Dewi You're a saint, Evan, a saint I tell you.

Dylan To the patron saint of the pint!

All *Iechyd da!*

> *Dewi stands and sings the Welsh National Anthem at the top of his lungs. The cast join in and belt out the anthem proudly. Lloyd and Will do not join in.*

Dewi
> *Mae hen wlad fy nhadau yn annwyl i mi,*
> *Gwlad beirdd a chantorion, enwogion o fri;*
> *Ei gwrol ryfelwyr, gwladgarwyr tra mâd,*
> *Tros ryddid gollasant eu gwaed.*
>
> *Gwlad, Gwlad, pleidiol wyf i'm gwlad,*
> *Tra môr yn fur i'r bur hoff bau,*
> *O bydded i'r heniaith barhau.*

> *The final note of the anthem is prolonged and then a blast of Arctic Monkeys, 'I Bet You Look Good on the Dancefloor' cuts across this. The cast thrash around and jump about and do the robot etc.*

> *Blackout.*

> *End of Act One.*

Act Two

SCENE ONE

10.30 p.m. Outside the Pavilion. Jess is roaring drunk now and shouting at the top of her lungs. Bethan and Mary try to quieten her.

Jess IT'S NOT COOOOL TO CLOSE OUR FUCKIN' SCHOOL!

Mary Shhh, Jess!

Jess IT'S NOT FUCKIN' COOL TO CLOSE OUR FUCKIN', SHITTY' FUCKIN' SCHOOOOOOOOL!

Mary Jess, shhhh!

Dylan and Big Nell are heading back inside with some chips.

Bethan Jess, seriously, keep it down will you?

Jess But it's not cool is it, sir?

Dylan No, Jessica, it is not.

Jess See, girls? Teacher says I'm right. It's not FUCKIN' COOL. Sir, tell them.

Dylan Not cool.

Jess At all, at all, at all.

Dylan Nope.

Jess Nope. It's shit, isn't it? Tell them.

Dylan It's really, really shit.

Jess Sir! You swore!

Dylan Oops.

Jess Oh sir, I love you.

Bethan Jess, stop!

Dylan I'm fond of you too, Jessica.

Jess I've had a bit to drink.

Dylan I can see that.

Bethan Jess!

Jess It's alright, he's cool. You're cool, aren't you, sir?

Big Nell He certainly is.

Jess He is, isn't he? Can I have a chip?

Big Nell Help yourself.

Jess Cheers, love. Truth be told I've always found Mr Thomas disturbingly sexy. A bit tubby round the middle, a bit dishevelled but in a *hot way*.

She shoves a load of chips in her mouth.

Bethan Oh Jesus Christ.

Jess (*laughs*) Are you blushing, sir? Are you?!

Big Nell (*amused*) Are you, Dylan?

Dylan I think I best go inside. See you on the dance floor, Nell?

Big Nell I'm coming now.

Jess We're having a girls' talk, sir. But don't you worry; you won't be dancing on your own, not while I still have breath. We'll be there now in a minute, throwing shapes alongside you like there's no tomorrow.

She throws some shapes in a drunken demonstration.

Dylan I look forward to it, Jessica. Don't think I've forgotten that essay you wrote on the Suffragettes, one of the best I've ever read. You were a talented student once and will be again, while I still have breath.

He laughs, exits.

Jess Aww, I love you, sir! (*To Big Nell.*) Don't worry, I'm not a threat, I'm only saying I think Mr Thomas is *awesome* and you two make a scorchin' couple, right?

Big Nell Thanks, I'm glad you approve.

Jess Seriously, I see wedding bells and babies. You heard it here first. Oh dear . . .

Big Nell What?

Jess Shouldn't have eaten those chips. (*She burps.*)

Big Nell Take her to the toilets quick!

Jess It's alright, I'll sober up a bit once I'm sick. Hold my hair for me, will you Beth?

Bethan Will do.

Bethan escorts Jess to the toilets. Big Nell exits. Mary stands outside having a smoke. Mark sidles up.

Mark Hi, Mary.

Mary I told you to stay away.

Mark It's not mine, Mary. I . . . I loved you too much for that.

Mary What I ever saw in you I cannot fathom.

Mark Well, for what it's worth I can still see everything I loved about you clear as day.

Mary It's worth nothing.

Mark You've grown cruel, Mary.

Mary What did you expect?

Mark We used to read together, do you remember?
You'd read to me, I'd read to you.

Mary Yeah, I remember.

Mark You dragged me into the library kicking and
screaming and shoved a book in my hand. My life
changed that day. The whole world opened up to me.
Thousands of adventures contained in one room and I've
been on all of them. I read and suddenly I'm somewhere
else, looking at everything through someone else's eyes.
I realise that they are me and I am them and we are all
connected.

I've never been anywhere, barely even left Wales, but I
feel like I've travelled all over . . . If I want to go to China
or India I just stick my nose in a book and I can smell the
spices in the air! I read all day long and when the book's
finished, I'm back here. I'm back here so I devour more
books. I eat them for breakfast, lunch and dinner. I chew
on those glorious words like jewels in my mouth, I digest
them and then what do I do? I spew them back up again.
Retching out diamonds as if they were nothing. As if they
were vomit. Because I don't have my own. Because I
don't have any of my own and I want . . . I really want . . .
I wanted to tell you –

Mary Reading about a place is a poor substitute to
actually going there, you fuckin' idiot.

Mark I know that, Mary, I do. But it's better than
nothing like. I would go, given half the chance . . . but
there's not been much work around lately.

Mary The bakery?

Mark Shut down a few years back.

Mary Shame.

Mark The whole town's been boarded up, have you seen?

Mary Yeah, I have.

Mark I've been on the dole.

Mary Oh?

Mark Well, they don't call it that. They have to keep the unemployment figures down, so they've created all these schemes. I'm volunteering . . . planting vegetables and selling them. No pay though.

Mary Right.

Mark Sneaky fuckers.

Mary Yes, they are.

Mark Still, you don't need to worry about any of this sort of thing now you've been to university and you're living in London, do you?

Mary Oh fuck off, Mark!

She exits.

Mark What? Mary? What did I say? Mary?!

SCENE TWO

10.30 p.m. Myfanwy stands inside the chip van as if she's on Juliet's balcony. Gary crouches outside the van looking up at her like Romeo.

Gary
But soft! What light through yonder chip van breaks?
It is the east, and Myfanwy is the sun.
Arise, fair sun, and kill the . . . the . . .

Myfanwy Envious moon.

Gary
                           . . . the envious moon.
Who is already sick to the back teeth,
That thou, her maid, art far more fit than she.

Myfanwy Ay me! (*She munches into a burger.*)

Gary
She speaks.
O, speak again, bright angel.

Myfanwy (*with her mouth full*)
O Romeo, Romeo! Wherefore art thou, Romeo?

Gary Not Romeo! Gary!

Myfanwy Gary, Gary, wherefore art thou?

Gary *I'm here, my cherub!* Give us a bite will you?

Myfanwy I'll do one better. You can have a burger of your very own. Perk of the job.

Gary Verily I shall accept said burger and I do give thee thanks.

Myfanwy You may kiss my hand.

   Gary kisses her hand. Myfanwy hands him his burger.

Gary Mmm, I could get used to this.

Myfanwy Want some chips to go with it?

Gary Nah. How about a song instead?

Myfanwy No, I'm shy.

Gary Ah come on. I've heard you sing loads of times.

Myfanwy When?

Gary Ya know . . . when you're workin' and that.

Myfanwy That's different.

Gary Why?

Myfanwy I'm singing to myself, no one's listening.

Gary I was listening.

Myfanwy You were spying.

Gary How do you expect to be a singer if you can't even sing for me like?

Myfanwy I don't expect to be one.

Gary You give up too easy. Maybe you never really wanted it that much to begin with.

Myfanwy I did too!

Gary Come on then!

Myfanwy I usually sing along to something.

Gary Stick a song on.

Myfanwy Okay . . . but promise me you won't laugh.

Gary I won't. I promise.

*Myfanwy turns on the stereo.She sings along to
'Laura' by Bat for Lashes. She sings along quietly with
her eyes closed at first but gradually gets louder and
louder until she sings with real passion. A dim light
appears above her that gradually gets brighter as the
song goes on. She has a beautiful voice. Men and
women come out of the shadows, pair up and slow
dance as she sings. Gary is spellbound.*

*As the song ends the light fades and the men and
women break apart and leave the stage. Silence.*

Myfanwy What do you think?

Gary Wow.

Myfanwy Really?

Gary You should enter *Britain's Got Talent*.

Myfanwy Nah. Shut up.

Gary No, actually, no, you're right. You're too good for that shitshow. You should be up there with the greats! I can see it now, your name in lights: Tom Jones, Shirley Bassey and Myfanwy Evans!

Myfanwy Thanks, Gary. (*She kisses his cheek.*)

Gary beams. An awkward moment. They get on with their work.

Blackout.

SCENE THREE

Music and Lights. 'Nightclubbing' by Iggy Pop. Big Nell moves amongst the dancers. The men and women begin to couple up as Nell's speech goes on.

Big Nell And so the night rolls on to all its inevitable conclusions. Is that romance in the air or simply lust and boredom? The silent pairing up of the last desperate men and women ready for the stumble home.

Pointing out a particularly drunk woman:

How many drinks till she's anybody's, do you think? One more I reckon.

She passes her a shot and the woman falls into the arms of the next man she sees.

All dolled up with no place to go but here. A sorry sight. A sad state of affairs by anyone's standards. The night will soon be over for him if he has any more.

The man she points to vomits all over himself and passes out.

Uh-oh, too late. With all the alcohol consumed it's a wonder anyone bothers. But still they try, possessed by drunken demons, they tongue and paw at one another, fall into bed and fail at the last hurdle to raise even a stirring. Brewer's droop: the mortal enemy of pissheads everywhere!

SCENE FOUR

Mark staggers outside. Bethan is holding on to a wall and puking.

Mark Oh, hi . . .

Bethan Hi.

She vomits.

Mark Ah Jesus, love, are you alright? You shouldn't be drinking in your condition.

Bethan I'm not. Morning sickness is not just in the morning.

Mark Oh . . . Listen I've been wanting to talk to you . . .

Bethan Yes?

Mark I was wondering . . . ?

Bethan It's not yours.

Mark Oh . . . I thought –

Bethan It's not yours, it's mine.

Mark Well yeah, but who's the –

Bethan It's mine.

Mark I'm sorry, Bethan.

Bethan I'm not. I should be but I'm not.

Mark Oh . . . Well, good then.

Bethan I love being pregnant. Everything seemed pointless before.

Mark Pointless . . . Yeah.

Bethan I have a reason now.

Mark I'm so sorry, Bethan . . . I should never –

Mary enters.

Mary Never what? (*Pause.*) I knew it.

Bethan Mary –

Mark I was drunk and she . . .

Mary She what?

Bethan Mary –

Mary If you dare lay any of the blame –

Mark No! No blame! It's just . . . she . . . looks so much like you nowadays.

Bethan Oh my God . . .

Silence. Mary stares at Mark, who looks away.

Mark That sounded really bad . . . I –

Mary Did you even use protection? Tell me you did and it broke. Please tell me that.

Mark No, I was –

Mary No. Of course you didn't! You never fuckin' do!

Jess enters.

Jess Mary, how long does it take to smoke a ciggie for fuck's sake?

She stops when she sees Mark.

Mark I was just leaving.

Jess Yes, I think you better or it's stilettos at dawn, you sleazy fuck!

Mark I'm sorry, Mary.

He exits hastily.

Jess Mary? Mary, what's up?

Mary Ask Bethan.

Bethan It's not his.

Jess OH, NO WAY!

Mary Bethan, tell the truth.

Bethan I am!

Jess It's his. Of course it's his. I'll castrate him!

Mary Why, Bethan? Why?

Bethan I was really drunk.

Jess Fuckin' hell.

Bethan Sorry, Jess. It's just . . . the lovely things he was saying . . . golden words like –

Jess Syrup. Words like great rivers of golden syrup.

Bethan He makes you feel like all the sweets in the shop are just for you.

Jess Give me a fag, will you?

Mary You don't smoke.

Jess I do now.

Bethan Don't! You gave up!

Jess Not now, Bethan, I'm having a moment. (*She lights up, coughs.*) Fuck me, this is absolutely revolting.

She carries on smoking regardless, gets out a hip flask, takes a swig and passes it to Mary.

Bethan I'm sorry, girls.

Jess Oh fuck it! Fuck all of it! We're supposed to be out havin' fun. It's the last Pavilion: a momentous occasion! Let's go and dance, eh? Drink some more and pull some hotties.

Mary Hotties round here? You need your eyes checked.

Jess Not from round here. A bit more exotic actually.

Mary Exotic?

Jess Bristol boys!

Bethan And they're fuckin' lush!

Jess Come on, Mary, live a little.

Mary Alright I'll have a dance.

Jess A dance and a snog. Get your best shimmies going, girls.

Bethan How's this for a shimmy?

Bethan shimmies at them. They laugh and exit shimmying into the dance hall. Music. The stage fills with drunken people dancing.

SCENE FIVE

Midnight. Lights up on Big Nell on the microphone atop the bar. Men and women surround the chip van like drunken zombies. Myfanwy and Gary serve them.

Big Nell The midnight stragglers descend on the chip van like zombies of the apocalypse ravenous for flesh. Unwanted and uncoupled, they make one last stab at getting a leg over, fill their faces with burger, give up and go home. 'Chips, glorious chips!' they cry, as they shovel them in; their faces bloodstained with ketchup. Burgers and hot dogs and onions: nothing quells the appetite quite like them. Nothing stifles the pangs of loneliness in quite the same way as a Styrofoam container of crispy yellow chips fresh out the fryer and dripping in grease. 'Yum, yum, yum in my tum!' they bellow and scoff into the night, like greedy little truffle pigs. And all salty and sexless they run 'wee, wee, weee' all the way home!

SCENE SIX

The dance floor. Music and lights. The men and women are now slow-dancing with one another to 'Time After Time' by Cyndi Lauper. Jess, Bethan and Mary dance with the Bristol boys. Jess dances provocatively. Will spots them on his way back from the toilets, and rushes into the bar.

Will Lloyd, I need you!

Lloyd What is it?

Will I need you! Now!

Big Nell Steady on, boys. I knew you two were close but not in public!

81

Everyone laughs.

Lloyd Shut your gob, fatso!

Dylan Insult my lover one more time, you cretinous little shit, you'll have me to deal with!

Will Lloyd!

Lloyd What?

Will They're dancing.

Lloyd What?

Dewi (*stands paralytic and slurs*) Comin' here and takin' our women! (*He collapses.*)

Lloyd Who?

Music cue: cross-fade into the beginning of 'Invaders Must Die' by The Prodigy on a loop like a heartbeat.

Will I don't recognise them.

Lloyd Are you thinkin' what I'm thinkin'?

Will I can smell them in the air, Lloyd.

Lloyd Me too, Will, me too. The unmistakable stench of *outsiders*.

Will Time to saddle up?

Lloyd Full Metal battle cry.

Both THIS IS MY FIST. THERE ARE MANY LIKE IT BUT THIS ONE IS MINE. WITHOUT ME IT IS USELESS. WITHOUT MY FISTS I AM USELESS.

Will Ready?

Lloyd Let's knock the thoughts right out of their eyes!

Will and Lloyd exit into the dance hall.

Dylan Oh Christ, here we go.

Big Nell Evan –

Evan You call the police. I'll get the mop.

The lights flash. Big Nell stands on top of the bar with the microphone. Will and Lloyd storm in with chairs from the bar to throw at the outsiders – a slow-motion fight ensues throughout Big Nell's speech. Lloyd and Will are vicious. The girls try to intervene but are thrown to the floor.

Big Nell At it they go! As ferocious as rabid dogs. Will and Lloyd: two peas in one very fucked-up pod. Heads as hard as bricks; vicious and vacuous in equal measure. The sickening dull thud of fists on bare skin, broken ribs and smashed faces. Howls of pain, teeth fly and bones splinter. Will and Lloyd: bathed in the glory of the fight and grinning horrible from ear to ear.

Powerhouses for one fleeting moment! Top dogs with broken bottles in hand! Kings of the shit heap! They'd tear them limb from limb if the sound of sirens didn't stop them. Those poor Bristol boys won't be coming back to Wales any time soon!

The music kicks in and the fight goes full speed. Evan and Dylan wade in and pull the boys apart, Big Nell grabs Will and gets him in a headlock, Dylan does the same to Lloyd. They march them into the bar. The sound of sirens. Evan exits with the Bristol boys.

SCENE SEVEN

Big Nell and Dylan drag the boys into the bar. They struggle.

Will Get off me, you fat bitch!

Dylan You watch your mouth, boy!

Lloyd Fuck off, old man!

Will This had got nothing to do with you, alright!

Lloyd Let us go!

Dylan Get them on to the floor, Nell.

Big Nell gets Will down on the floor on his stomach. Dylan gets Lloyd down next to him.

Dewi Well done, boys! You showed 'em! They won't show their faces round here again.

Big Nell Shut it you, or you're cut off!

Dewi Oop zipped, Nelly love. Word is my bond.

Evan enters.

Evan They've gone. I told the police you two had scarpered. The Bristol boys have been taken to A&E.

Big Nell Why you continue to protect them is beyond me! They don't deserve it, Evan.

Evan They've got nothing, love.

Dylan and Big Nell get off the boys.

Lloyd Why can't you mind your own business, you interfering old fuck?!

Will We could have had 'em!

Big Nell Was there not enough damage done?!

Lloyd Nowhere near!

Big Nell What is wrong with you both?! Can not one Friday night pass by without incident?! Do you want to end up in prison?

Will Fuck you! Fuck off! We could of had –

Big Nell You could have killed that boy!

Dylan Lock the doors, Evan, it's time for an intervention. This has gone on long enough.

Evan Ah, Dyl man. Come on. I don't want no bother.

Dylan LOCK THE DOORS.

Evan locks the doors. Cross-fade to the toilets.

SCENE EIGHT

Jess paces the bathroom screaming at the top of her lungs. Bethan and Mary look on bewildered.

Jess Aaarrrrrrgh!!

Mary Jess?!

Jess Aaaaaaaaaaaaargh!

Mary Jess, calm down!

Jess Fuuuucccccckkkkkk!

She punches the wall. And claws at her face and clothes.

Bethan Jess, stop!

Jess I gotta get out! I have to! I have to! I can't breathe! I can't breathe! I'll die if I don't get out. I'll die.

The girls grab hold of her in an embrace from either side. She sobs.

Mary Alright. It's alright, Jess.

Bethan Shhh now, lovely, it's okay.

Jess I don't want this life. I don't want it. I don't want it. There has to be more. There has to. Take me with you back to London, Mary.

Mary I can't Jess. I –

Jess Why not?!

Mary I don't have the room. I would let you, honestly, it's just –

Jess Please, Mary! I won't be in your way.

Mary I live in a bedsit, Jess. You can sit on the bed and cook your dinner at the same time.

Jess But you're working.

Mary London . . . It's not how you imagine it . . . it's expensive.

Jess But you have a good job.

Mary It's not that good. I earn a tenner an hour if I'm lucky.

Jess That's loads!

Mary Not in London.

Bethan What do you mean, if you're lucky?

Mary It changes. Week to week. Day to day sometimes.

Bethan How come?

Mary I'm a temp.

Bethan A what?

Mary I work through an agency. I haven't got a proper job. I'm not what you think I am. I'm not special, I'm not successful. I'm not . . .

Bethan But I thought . . .

Mary I know.

Bethan You got a degree –

Mary I got a Master's as well.

Jess So what are you doing?

Mary I'm in London stapling bits of paper together.

Jess No, be serious.

Mary Filing and filing whole rainforests of paper *bollocks* for no discernible reason. Warehouses full of archived crap that's never looked at again. I am fuckin' living the dream, girls!

Bethan A temp . . .

Mary Every day I go into a different office where I know no one.

Bethan But you got a distinction . . .

Mary I can't even get my foot through the door for an interview. Bethan, I'm a fraud.

Jess At least you've got a job, Mary. Christ, you don't know how lucky you are. I'd kill for a job like that. I'd've liked to go to university too, you know!

Mary Jess, I'm doing a job a monkey could do. I don't even need my degree.

Jess But you got one, Mary! Three glorious years of study and fun away from here learning about life – it sounds like paradise to me.

Mary Then go.

Jess How would I ever pay back that kind of money, Mary?! You've become a real Londoner, you know that?

Mary What's that supposed to mean?

Jess Myopic.

Mary is taken aback.

That's right. I know some big words too!

Mary I'm not sure myopic means what you think it means . . .

Jess gives her a filthy look.

Never mind.

Jess Alright, I mean you've turned into a self-absorbed, self-important bitch with her nose in the air.

Mary In which case 'myopic' is a poorly chosen word and you should've opted for conceited, narcissistic, or egotistical.

Jess Oh fuck you the fuck right off, alright?

Bethan Stop it! Both of you!

Silence.

Mary Sorry, Jess.

Jess I'm failing anyway. No point studying for exams to go and work in a supermarket, is there?

Mary Maybe not, fair do's.

Bethan Sorry to party-poop but I'm knackered, girls.

Mary Yeah, me too. Call it a night?

Jess Fuck yes! Cut our losses.

They gather up their handbags.

Mary Jess?

Jess Yeah?

Mary Alright then.

Jess What?

Mary When I go back, you can come with me.

Jess Really?

Mary Yeah.

Jess But really, really?

Mary Yes! We'll sleep top-to-toe cosy.

Jess Like when we were little.

Mary A trial run. I'm sure you're just as capable of stuffing envelopes as all the graduates.

Jess Oh my God! Thank you! Thank you so much!

Mary I'll be glad of the company, to be honest. London is a lonely place.

Jess OH MY GOLLY FUCKIN' GOSH! LONDON! Give me a ciggie.

Bethan Jess!

Jess Not now, Bethan, I'm having a moment. I need to feel the sweet sting of cigarette smoke in my lungs!

Jess and Mary exit laughing, leaving Bethan alone for a moment. She looks down at her belly and strokes it.

Bethan Hurry up, eh?

SCENE NINE

Back in the bar.

Dylan Last week it was who?

Big Nell That lot from Builth.

Dylan The week before?

Big Nell That black lad David.

Dylan And before that?

Big Nell Skag heads and that Polish chap.

Dylan And on and on, you get my drift.

Will So what?

Lloyd Yeah, so what?

Dylan What is your beef, boys? Why all this hatred? Where is your love for your fellow man? Where is your compassion? Your empathy? Tell me.

Lloyd I don't know what you're on about. Yabber yabber is all I hear. Drone and roar and on and on, you get *my* drift?

Dylan You've no respect for your elders, no respect for your peers, for yourselves or for the country that birthed you.

Will I don't know about you, but it was my mother squeezed me out.

Dylan But it's Wales that gives you your identity.

Lloyd I don't give a fuck about Wales.

Dylan You're not looking close enough. You need to get your head out of the pint glass and take a look around you.

Lloyd What at?

Will Yeah, at what exactly?

Dylan How often do you boys leave this town behind you and escape into the hills? It's all there in that anthem you don't know the words to. Get up into those mountains, sink your hands into the soil, embrace the land cos it's ours and it's the one thing that can never be taken away from us. Feel proud to be a part of it.

Lloyd Smear our faces in sheep shit and dance around the bonfire!

Dylan I understand your anger, boys, but it's misdirected, see. You should be joining the Welsh Assembly and bussing up to London to protest but instead you stay here and fight your own people: young boys in the same predicament as you. It has to stop. You hear me? It must.

Big Nell I'm signing you up. We'll go together.

Lloyd We're not going anywhere. You're fucked in the head you are.

Dylan William?

Will shakes his head but says nothing. Lloyd grabs a pint glass and raises it in his fist above Evan's head, threateningly. Will grabs a chair.

Lloyd Let us out of here now before I glass someone! I'm sick of listening to this shite!

Evan Alright, lads. Alright.

Lloyd Unlock that fuckin' door now or I'll slice your face.

Dylan Calm down, Lloyd. If you want to slice anyone it's me, not Evan, you know that.

Lloyd That's right, it is!

Evan Don't! I'm getting the keys.

Lloyd Now get this into your thick skull, old man. I'll never go anywhere with you, see? *Never.* Not to London, not anywhere – this is my town. I know my place and this is it. I don't need your help to see anything. I know my place.

Evan (*unlocks the door*) You're free to go.

Lloyd exits.

Will Sorry, Dylan . . . Evan.

Dylan Will you come with us, William?

Will Can't.

Dylan Why not?

Will Can't, that's all.

Will exits.

Big Nell You tried, Dyl.

Dylan The waste. The sheer waste.

Evan Last round's on me.

Dewi Last round? Already? By God does time fly when you're pissing it up the wall.

Cross-fade to chip van.

SCENE TEN

Gary and Myfanwy are packing things away in the chip van.

Myfanwy How'd your first night on the job go?

Gary It was great! Did I do alright?

Myfanwy You were brilliant. I'll put a word in with the boss.

Gary Thanks.

Myfanwy Here's your wages.

Gary Wow. Thanks. I'll save it up for our date.

Myfanwy You're too sweet for your own good, you are.

Gary You mean stupid.

Myfanwy No, sweet. I hope you stay that way. It's lovely.

Gary grins, sheepish.

Myfanwy We're all done here. You can go home now, I'll pack up. Same time next week?

Gary Oh no, I'll walk you home.

Myfanwy There's no need.

Gary Miv, the town is crawling with drunkards, what kind of man would I be if I let you brave the streets alone?

Myfanwy (*laughs*) Oh alright. You've worn me down.

Gary Yes!

She starts to tidy stuff away. Gary helps. Cross-fade back to the bar.

SCENE ELEVEN

Catrin enters the bar. She is drunk, and very worked up.

Big Nell You have got / to be fuckin' jokin'.

Catrin You failed. Your petition failed! That's what I came to tell you!

Dylan We're not supposed to find out till Monday.

Catrin Did you really think six hundred signatures would make a difference? They have to save twenty-seven million in three years. You're all living in cloud cuckoo land.

Big Nell (*screams at her*) Get out!

Catrin You all act like this is personal! I'm just doing my job and you persecute me for it. I can't leave my house without people shouting at me on the street!

Big Nell Aw, my heart bleeds.

Catrin It's not just the school, the library is closing, this place is closing. It's happening. It's happening and there's nothing you or I or anyone else can do about it. But if you would just do your job and *please* stop forcing my hand, then maybe I –

Dylan rounds on her.

Dylan I do my job! I work sixty-hour weeks doing my job and then I come for a night out with my mates and you're fuckin' here waitin' for me!

Catrin I work long hours too, Dylan.

Dylan I don't doubt it, Catrin. I'm sure you do. But with all due respect you only just got here and you're inexperienced.

Catrin I AM SICK TO DEATH –

Dylan You're green! You're wet behind the ears! You haven't seen the decline of the poorest kids in the classroom over the last six years! Teachers have it hard but it's nothing compared to those children! Classrooms full of kids who think they'll never be able to afford university so why bother to study for GCSEs. That believe the best they can hope for is an apprenticeship for three pound an hour with no job at the end of it.

Catrin Then it's up to you, the teachers, to encourage them to apply themselves and take out loans if they have to.

Dylan Oh I know. I know it is. It's one of the many uphill battles we're facing daily but that's not the worst of it. No. The worst and most unforgivable thing I have to observe every day of my teaching life, is children who can't concentrate because they're *starving*; surviving on one school meal a day sometimes.

Catrin And that's my fault too, is it?!

Dylan Children with severe depression, whose parents have had their benefits cut, whose parents have been sanctioned and are relying on charity. Kids who come to school in worn-out clothes, whose shoes are too small for them, kids that are so malnourished their teeth are falling out their heads! Every class there's ten or eleven of them. That's a third of them, Catrin. A *third*. There's no teacher training that can help you to cope with that. I can't cope with it . . . I can't. (*He chokes back tears.*) So you're *fuckin' right* we're in special measures! You try taking an exam when you've barely eaten in two days.

Catrin Student numbers are dropping, surplus places cost money –

Dylan Money, money. Yeah, yeah, yeah I know. But I don't see numbers, I see children. Have you talked with any of them? Taught them? Got to know them?

Catrin . . .

Dylan They're bright and difficult and imaginative and a *pain in the arse* and brilliantly funny and they deserve better. They deserve an education I can't give them! Party politics makes its way into my classroom because I need my students to understand why they are suffering. They need to know that despite what the papers say it's not their parents' fault. They need to understand how the odds are stacked against them so that they can overcome them. And if all that's outside the curriculum so be it. So if you need to fire me then I suggest you fucking do it.

Big Nell No, Dyl.

Dylan It's alright, love.

Catrin It's not that I want to . . .

Dylan I know.

Catrin I have to let seven teachers go.

Dylan It must be very difficult.

Catrin It is. It really is. I . . . I can't sleep.

Dylan Enough of the hand-wringing, just get it over with, will you?

Catrin You're fired with immediate effect.

She exits. Silence.

Dewi You told her, Dylan.

Big Nell Are you alright?

Dylan Felt good to finally say it.

Evan What now?

Dylan (*weary*) We keep protesting. We won't go down without a fight. That's the Welsh way.

Evan We'll be there.

Dewi That's right.

Dylan *Diolch.*

Dewi Lock-in, Evan?

Evan Not tonight. I'm beat.

Dewi But it's the last one.

Evan Oh yeah . . . I keep forgettin'.

Dewi One for the road, eh? Do not go gentle into that good night.

Evan Alright. One more.

Evan and Big Nell pour everyone a pint.

How's about a poem, Dewi?

Dewi What you say?

Dylan Ah yes, give us a poem, Dew. A Dylan Thomas.

Dewi Ah a poem . . . a poem . . . right you are.

He stands and straightens up, takes a deep breath and recites beautifully and with real depth of feeling the first verse of 'Fern Hill' by Dylan Thomas as if he's spoken it a thousand times, like muscle memory.

Dewi
Now as I was young and easy under the apple boughs
About the lilting house and happy as the grass was
    green,
The night above the dingle starry,
Time let me hail and climb
Golden in the heydays of his eyes.

The scenes now start to overlap as we cross-fade back to the chip van.

SCENE TWELVE

Myfanwy is locking up the van.

Gary Miv?

Myfanwy Yes?

Dewi
And as I was green and carefree, famous among the
    barns
About the happy yard and singing as the farm was
    home,
In the sun that is young once only –

Gary When I walk you home . . .

Myfanwy Yes?

Gary Can I hold your hand like?

Dewi
Time let me play and be
Golden in the mercy of his means . . .

Myfanwy Yeah, okay.

Gary Ah, this is the best night ever!

Lloyd and Will approach the chip van.

Lloyd Not so fast. We want chips.

Myfanwy Oh sorry, lads, we're just closing.

Lloyd So open up again.

Myfanwy Everything's been put away.

Will But we're hungry.

Myfanwy I'd have to turn the fryer back on, it would take ages . . .

Gary Yeah, come on, lads, it's late, be reasonable.

Myfanwy Gary, shush.

The fear sinks in.

Lloyd What did you say to me, boy?

Myfanwy Don't start, Lloyd, alright? He's just a child.

Will Let the boy speak, Myfanwy.

Lloyd Yeah, come on, boy. You were saying?

Gary I was saying . . . I was saying . . . be . . . be reasonable.

Will He's a cheeky little shit, isn't he?

Lloyd Yeah. I'm not sure I like your tone, Gary. I'm not sure I like your face either.

Gary My face?

Will Yeah, maybe we should do some rearranging. What do you reckon, Lloyd?

Gary I rise up . . . up . . . up. Floating at first, looking down on the furious little creatures moving below. I see myself lying very, very still. I'm leaving. Leaving it all behind me. Ascending up into the safety of the black bandaged night. My blood gushes around me soft and warm as velvet. Speeding up faster and faster. Beam me up! Let's get out of this place! I've reached escape velocity. Twenty-five thousand miles per hour! Seven miles per second! I've enough kinetic energy to escape the pull of the earth's gravity completely. Here I go! Up into the darkness. Up into the great beyond. Straight through the earth's atmosphere and up among the stars. Bouncing between planets. Whizzing through the night. Nothing but star dust now but that's all I ever was anyway. All any of us are.

Evan
　　Nothing I cared, in the lamb white days, that time
　　　　would take me –

Will
　　Up to the swallow thronged loft by the shadow of my
　　　　hand –

Lloyd
　　In the moon that is always rising –

Gary I look back down and see myself lying in a pool of red. I feel giddy. I feel travel sick. I want to come back down but I'm so high up. I want to go back down to my sister and Myfanwy and Wales and all its violent beauty and muddy misery. It may be damaged and desolate but it's my home town. I love it despite its faults. I love my home and the people in it.

Dylan
　　Nor that riding to sleep
　　I should hear him fly with the high fields –

Mary

And wake to the farm forever fled from the childless
land.

Gary How did this happen? Why did it? I watch the boys
that are beating me to the brink of my life and I want to
reach out and touch their cold hearts and nurse them
back to health. But it's too late. Too late for them. Too
late for me.

Bethan

Oh as I was young and easy in the mercy of his
means –

Gary I'm not done yet. I'm not finished. I'd only just
begun! I drift further and further away. I'm so far away
from myself now I'm just a speck of blood in the distance,
nothing more.

Jess

Time held me green and dying –

Myfanwy

Though I sang in my chains like the sea.

Gary I'm disappearing. Out on the edge of sight. Going.
Going. Gone.

*The sound of sirens in the distance. The lights fade
slowly.*

The End.